I have had the privilege to enjoy the words of wisdom from Sister Connie in her previous writings (*God's Plan for Our Success, Nehemiah's Way; The Elijah Anointing;* and *Your Holy Spirit Arsenal*). I have also read this book on healing. I am thankful for her heart of passion for Christ and His church.

I believe her sensitivity to the Holy Spirit has given her spiritual insight concerning the subject of healing. I am believing this book will be used to bring freedom to many who have struggled to receive their miracle. Connie's willingness to share God's truths is inspiring and encouraging.

Sit back and begin to enjoy the labor of this mighty woman of God, and prepare to be encouraged, renewed, and healed in the mighty name of Jesus.

RON RUSSELL
Senior Pastor
PTC Ministries
Connersville, Indiana

Be Healed!

DESTINY IMAGE BOOKS BY CONNIE HUNTER-URBAN

Your Holy Spirit Arsenal
God's Plan for Our Success, Nehemiah's Way

Be Healed!

*Secrets to Divine Healing
in the Model of Jesus*

Connie Hunter-Urban

DESTINY IMAGE® PUBLISHERS, INC.

P.O. Box 310, Shippensburg, PA 17257-0310

"Promoting Inspired Lives."

This book and all other Destiny Image and Destiny Image Fiction books are available at Christian bookstores and distributors worldwide.

Cover design by Eileen Rockwell

Interior design by Terry Clifton

For more information on foreign distributors, call 717-532-3040.

Reach us on the Internet: www.destinyimage.com.

ISBN 13 TP: 978-0-7684-4841-2

ISBN 13 eBook: 978-0-7684-4842-9

ISBN 13 HC: 978-0-7684-4844-3

ISBN 13 LP: 978-0-7684-4843-6

For Worldwide Distribution, Printed in the U.S.A.

1 2 3 4 5 6 7 8 / 23 22 21 20 19

Acknowledgments

I want to thank:

My heavenly Father for downloading this assignment into me, sending me on this journey, helping me along the way, and healing me in the process.

- My mother in-law Joan, who passed during the writing of this book. Her encouragement was never-ending.

- My husband, Wade, who supports me physically and spiritually.

- My parents, Ernest and Audrey Hunter, who demonstrated Jesus' principles of healing each day of my life.

- My children and grandchildren who allowed me to exercise my faith genes throughout their lives.

- My close friends who are constantly supportive—Margie, Curtis, Sheryl, Sharon, Amanda, Karla, Sarah.

Contents

Foreword

SEVERAL YEARS AGO, A PASTOR'S WIFE, "KIM," TOLD ME A STORY I've never forgotten. Moving from Texas to Colorado Springs to assume their pastorate meant buying a new house and vehicle. One day, she drove home with her two daughters in her first Colorado snowstorm, and they found themselves sliding into a deep ditch. They were stuck. How would they get out? How long would it take? Who would help them? Suddenly, Kim looked down and remembered she was driving their new four-wheel-drive SUV. She reached down and engaged the gears then stepped on the gas. Immediately, they were out of the ditch, back on the road, and headed toward home.

I know many people today who find themselves or someone they love in deep ditches with various health concerns. They're stuck and discouraged, wondering where they can go to find help or if this is the way it will always be. How will they get out? How long will it take? Who will help them?

Decades ago, healing for sicknesses of all kinds could be found in the Body of Christ. Men and women around the world put legs on their faith and walked into the lives of people in need. They dared to take God at His Word, lay hands on the infirmed, and speak healing over them in Jesus' name. When my parents faced sickness and other kinds of needs, they had two pastors they knew would help pray the prayer of faith. That's where our burgeoning family headed in our green Ford station wagon many times when we found ourselves in need. We tarried with these faith giants and received our answers there.

Unfortunately, this kind of faith is far rarer today. Lack of use has caused the healing gift to atrophy, and the ability and confidence to access healing power has been largely lost for many in the Body of Christ. Most of us would find it difficult to think of two pastors, two friends, two leaders, or any other person who knows how to pray that desperate prayer of faith.

That's why this book is so needed. In John 14:12, Jesus told us that greater works than He did, we would do. Connie helps us to clearly examine what Jesus, the Great Healer, did and how He did it so we can learn to do it, too. We need it for ourselves and our families as well as for others facing grave illnesses. We must teach and demonstrate and keep the healing gift alive, active, and well-used for future generations. What greater way to lift up Christ than for His followers to duplicate His works? The world is waiting and ready for the sons of God to be made manifest (see Rom. 8:19).

They're waiting and ready, and so should we be. Connie shows us how to do that by teaching us the healing principles of Jesus—learn, examine, remember, then go out and do what Jesus did, say what Jesus said, then see the results that Jesus saw.

LYNDA HUNTER-BJORKLUND
Christian Author and Speaker

Prologue

In September 2015, I was in Oklahoma City on babysitting duty for my granddaughter while my daughter started back to work. During that stay filled with diapers, formula, and a million kisses to our three-month-old treasure, the Lord spoke into my spirit: "I'm sending you on another book journey." I was excited. I hadn't written for a while, and writing is when I'm most fulfilled. However, though I eagerly awaited His assignment about the topic, He didn't tell me what I was to write. When I left my daughter's house in October and headed home to Indiana, I had a couple days before Wade and I flew to Europe to preach. When we returned, the rest of the year was too chaotic to dwell much on my new book.

Then 2016 arrived with much busyness but still no book assignment. I jumped into regular ministry duties—newsletters, streaming, blogs, individual ministry, services. Wade and I were also speaking and traveling extensively for ministry. Then, during this time, I got my book direction through a dream—I was to write about healing. I loved it! This divine commission was the clearest of all my prior writing assignments. I was also very familiar with this subject because I'd operated in a healing ministry since I was young. I continued other ministry duties while I assembled notes for the new book.

A few days later, my writing was progressing when I caught the first virus. No problem. I taught in public school for thirty-three years and had my share of bugs. This time, though, before I recuperated, I caught something else then something else and grew sicker. A few weeks later, I was diagnosed with pneumonia. That's when I thought about the irony of my writing a book on healing. I questioned my new assignment when I became sicker and couldn't find victory. How could I tell others about healing if I wasn't grabbing it for myself? Although I knew He'd clearly directed me, I'd determined to give up and hadn't worked on the book for a couple days when Holy Spirit spoke gently into my heart: "Why do you think you're getting attacked?" As He reminded me that the enemy comes to discourage and derail, His words clarified my book's purpose. I dug in and kept going, even as I worsened over the next few months. I pressed ahead, and this book is the result.

During my healing book journey, I've learned much to impart to my readers and to apply to myself and my family's needs. When the Lord directed me to write about healing, He said to study Jesus' examples and compare how different gospels treat each story. Every one of those precious accounts provides principles to apply to a healing ministry or to our own healing needs. In this book, I'll share His stories, principles to glean from them, and lessons I learned during my 2016 trials. In these pages, I hope you can find your own healing through His examples and learn how to use what He taught to appropriate healing for yourself and others. You can have victory when you learn the lessons of the miracles.

Chapter One

Healings and Miracles

AT ONE OF OUR REVIVAL MEETINGS, GOD REVEALED THAT SANDY had a growth in her stomach. Knowing the importance of a positive witness, she hadn't shared her need with others but told the Lord she believed He'd heal her. She asked Him to reveal her problem to someone. A few days later at our service, Holy Spirit revealed the issue. When we prayed, anointing fell mightily, and she was slain in the Spirit. As she lay on the floor, something happened in her body, and pain left. A couple weeks later, though, symptoms returned. Instead of allowing fear and doubt to ocreep in, she set her jaw and asserted, "No way! I got my healing; I'm not givin' it back." By refusing the illness' return, symptoms left immediately and haven't returned in over twenty years.

Although miracles happen regularly today, sometimes God chooses not to heal immediately but through a longer process. We'd all like immediate freedom from pain and no more symptoms, but God has a plan and a timing for everything. Perhaps He wants to demonstrate His might to someone who needs to get saved. Maybe He wants to teach something—trust in Him, patience, perseverance. Healing is His will, so you should believe in His wisdom for how it will be accomplished. Healings and miracles, although different, are both part of God's plan for His kids.

What Did Jesus Do?

After Jesus and His disciples had experienced a second miracle of feeding a crowd, this time of 4,000 (see Mark 8:1-9), He and His disciples left in a boat to the region of Dalmanutha. There, Pharisees accosted Him, so He again travelled by boat to the lake's other side (see Mark 8:11-13). Then Mark tells a story that happened later at Bethsaida but which other gospels don't mention. People brought a blind man to Jesus and begged Him to touch the man (see Mark 8:22-26). Jesus didn't heal him immediately but took him by the hand and led him out of town. Then, He spat on the blind man's eyes and put His hands on him. After Jesus touched him, He asked the man if he saw anything. The blind man looked up and said, "I see men like trees, walking" (Mark 8:24). He again laid His hands on the eyes and made him look up. The man's sight was fully restored; he saw everyone clearly. Jesus sent him back to his house, telling him not to go to town or tell anyone in town.

Healings or Miracles?

The New Testament's first reference to Jesus' healings and miracles tells He travelled around Galilee preaching, teaching, and healing all kinds of sickness and disease (see Matt. 4:23). To accomplish this, He usually performed miracles, but the blind man's narrative demonstrates that miracles and healings differ and that miracles aren't the only way He healed. When Paul lists gifts of the Spirit, gifts of healings and working of miracles are separate because they're different (see 1 Cor. 12:9-10). Miracles happen instantly while healings occur over time, as a process, and often with multiple prayers. Jesus prayed for Peter's mother-in-law, stood over her, touched her hand, and rebuked the fever. It left, and she rose and served (see Luke 4:39; Matt. 8:15). That was a miracle. After Jesus healed the Syro-Phoenician woman's daughter, they arrived home and the daughter was still in bed (see Mark 7:30). That was a healing that needed time for completion. In the Old Testament, Hezekiah grew sick, and God told Isaiah he would die. Hezekiah turned his face toward the wall and cried to God, who then told Isaiah He'd heal Hezekiah. He was healed but wasn't able to go out until the third day (see 2 Kings 20:5-7). Sometimes a time gap exists between your prayer and its fulfillment.

This blind man's story represents a healing. After He prayed, Jesus asked the man what he saw. His response shows how a progressive healing works—he saw men, but they were unclear and resembled walking trees. Although miracles usually occur in our services, sometimes we witness responses similar to the blind man's words—they're better but not totally well. Healing has begun but isn't finished. When that happens, neither the prayer partner nor afflicted person should be discouraged because not every prayer is answered with a miracle. Often, like Jesus and the blind man, if you pray again, healing will be accomplished, but sometimes it takes even longer. That doesn't mean the end result is less authentic than with a miracle; they're different processes. Jesus alluded to this distinction in His hometown when He couldn't do miracles or mighty works, just some healings (see Mark 6:5). We all would prefer a miracle, but sometimes His work is done as a progression.

Paul compares the process of sowing and reaping to getting answers: "what you sow, you do not sow that body that shall be, but mere grain—perhaps wheat or some other grain. But God gives it a body as He pleases, and to each seed its own body" (1 Cor. 15:37-38). Sowing isn't about what you see as you plant but about what that seed will become. An acorn doesn't look like an oak tree nor an apple seed like the fruit tree it will become. Similarly, when you sow your prayer and watch the process begin, the seed doesn't look very impressive, not like the eventual healing. However, after you plant that seed of faith, restoration has begun. As you water it with prayer and faith, you'll see evidence pushing through. Even then, though, it's not complete. You must wait for the full process because in due season the promised harvest will come forth. God created your body to heal over time—cuts repair, broken bones mend, white cells fight infection, organs kill sick cells. Often, supernatural healing requires time, too.

Symptoms

After a healing or miracle, the enemy usually tries to convince you that you didn't receive it. If Jesus gives a healing, only you can return that gift. Even with miracles, which occur immediately, symptoms often take time to leave. During that time, some people lose their healing because they believe symptoms instead of the healing, give up, and say they weren't healed when they're just experiencing residual symptoms, not the disease. Jonah calls those "worthless idols" or "lying vanities" (Jon. 2:8 NKJV, KJV) because you believe those lies instead of God's mercy. The devil was/is a liar and "murderer from the beginning...there is no truth in him. When he speaks a lie, he speaks from his own resources [not God's], for he is a liar and the father of it" (John 8:44). His character and purpose are to deceive, so he can't be truthful. Therefore, when he tries to convince you to reject your healing, don't believe that lie.

When I was young, we horrified kids freaked out as our grandmother chopped the heads off chickens. They were dead, but those heads still flopped around like they were alive. Although illness is dying in your body, you get freaked out while symptoms are flopping around like they're still operating. They're no longer viable, so don't be preoccupied with symptoms. Even if you experienced immediate freedom from pain but symptoms later return, don't buy into the lie. You can be healed but still feel sick as restoration becomes complete. Look to the Healer and believe in the healing. Don't allow satan to turn victory into defeat. Once unbelief comes, he has a foothold because his only dominion over you is what you give him. Voicing words that you didn't receive your healing negates it. Symptoms say you're not healed, but God says you are. Although healing is in progress, symptoms like pain and weakness may still be part of your body's nature.

The enemy wants you to relinquish your healing, so he uses symptoms to make a mockery of the healing and trick you into believing it was false. He wants you to be in pain, suffering, and bondage to whatever he throws at you, especially sickness. He has plans for you—to steal, kill, and destroy you physically, mentally, emotionally, and spiritually (see John 10:10). If he can't kill you physically, he'll try other types of destruction, like murdering your reputation or belittling your integrity. The devil may have lied about, harassed, and even tried to kill you; he didn't accomplish your destruction because you're an overcomer with Jesus' authority. He came to destroy the devil's works (see 1 John 3:8), so giving the battle to Him changes the enemy's plans. The Bible says to "submit to God. Resist the devil and he will flee from you" (James 4:7). Resist the devil's ploys because symptoms can derail God's purpose. If you simply say, "You ain't the boss o' me!" he turns and runs. Then the Lord uses those attacks for your promotion and preparation for the next season.

Laying On of Hands

The laying on of hands brings powerful healings and miracles. In many of Jesus' stories, the sick desperately shouted for Him, pressed in, and approached Him for His touch. In this scenario, others brought the man for Jesus' touch. This is part of an intercessor's role. When you're sick or have a long-time ailment like the man's blindness, you can become spiritually and physically tired; getting victory is difficult. Then, you need prayer partners who understand His touch's power. He knows your human frailties and willingly touches you, even if approaching Him is initiated by others. Once, intercessors brought those with various diseases. He laid hands on them and healed them (see Luke 4:40-41). Jesus enumerated a healing prescription:

> *These signs will follow those who believe: In My name they will cast out demons; they will speak with new tongues; they will take up serpents; and if they drink anything deadly, it will by no means hurt them; they will lay hands on the sick, and they will recover* (Mark 16:17-18).

This passage contains much wealth. First, experiencing signs and wonders is simple—believe. Then, pray in His name to appropriate His authority, even over demons. Because Holy Spirit knows how to pray when you don't, use your prayer language. You're protected from whatever comes along—serpents, poisons, sickness. This means anything that stings, is poisonous, or has venom—including others' words. But this promise also has an implied message: Use wisdom and don't purposely subject yourself to dangerous things. However, when you are exposed, faith says you're exempt from natural dangers like snake venom, bee stings, spider or scorpion bites, and poisons. Finally, the laying on of hands is a great part of the process for recovery.

Jesus healed through His hands often. Once, blind men cried out for healing then followed Him into a house. After He asked if they believed and they confirmed, He touched their eyes, and they were opened (see Matt 9:27-30). The lady in the temple who was bent over for eighteen years straightened up as soon as He laid hands on her (see Luke 13:13). After people begged Him to put His hand on a deaf man with a speech impediment, Jesus took him aside, put His fingers in his ears, spat, and touched his tongue. He then looked to heaven and commanded the ears and tongue to operate. They were immediately healed (see Mark 7:32-35). Another time, though disciples scolded people for bringing children (Luke 18:15 says "infants"), He loved them and laid hands on them (see Matt. 19:13-15). Jairus told Jesus to "Come and lay Your hands on [his sick daughter], that she may be healed, and she will live" (Mark 5:23). Laying on of hands was part of Jesus' healing power to infuse into others. Whether He took the dead girl's hand, touched the blind man's eyes, or laid His hands on multitudes (see Luke 8:54; Mark 8:25; Luke 4:40), Jesus healed through His touch.

Just as the Great Healer laid His hands on those needing to be healed, His disciples also healed by their hands' touch (see Acts 14:3). As disciples chose Stephen and others for leadership, they brought candidates "before the apostles; and...laid hands on them" to activate powerful ministries (Acts 6:6-7). When Publius' father was sick with fever and dysentery, Paul laid hands on him, prayed, and healed him. Then, the island's other inhabitants with diseases flocked to him and were healed (see Acts 28:8-9). Like first century leaders followed Jesus' example of laying on of hands, that practice should be common today. Holy Spirit's touch comes through human hands working as His hands to bring His healing into bodies. That power gets kicked into gear when we, as transfer agents, lay hands upon someone to impart healing anointing and allow Holy Spirit's power to infuse into his/her body.

David said, "Blessed be the Lord my Rock, who trains my hands for war, and my fingers for battle" (Ps. 144:1). Your hands and fingers are crucial in the healing battle. Your fingers anoint with oil; then you lay on hands to activate healing. They're both part of your healing equipment but also important as you raise them to worship, to help those in need, or to volunteer instead of expecting others to do all the work. "Less glamorous" jobs are part of your training because they teach essential lessons healing warriors will need. The former shepherd boy understood this concept from personal experience. Even common uses of your hands are part of your training to become mighty men and women of valor who will shepherd others.

Look Up!

Another lesson from this passage is that if you want to be healed, change your focus. The first time Jesus prayed, the blind man was looking down. After laying hands on him again, Jesus "made him look up" (Mark 8:25). The word for *look up* is *anablepo*. It means "look up; by implication to recover sight."[1] Many are blinded by the world (see 2 Cor. 4:4); looking up at Jesus brings clarity, sight, and vision. After the man looked up, healing was completed. If you want your vision to change, adjust where you're looking—shift your attention from earth's reality to what's yours in Kingdom reality. If your vision isn't focused on Jesus, you're looking in the wrong place. Too often vision is directed on the earth's dust, i.e. man. Jesus should be whom you seek first; instead, people investigate everything the world offers *before* looking to Jesus. However, that doesn't mean you shouldn't use wisdom or do everything humanly possible to stay well or get better. Many physical ailments are because of choices or not using common sense—you've neglected a wholesome diet or adequate exercise, practiced habits that hurt your body, drunk after someone who's sick, or erratically washed your hands. Many abuse their bodies even though Holy Spirit considers it His temple in which to dwell (see 1 Cor. 6:19).

The Bible shows the importance of using wisdom about the body. David and his hungry men ate the showbread though Hebrew law prohibited it. Jonathan's hunger affected his effectiveness in battle, so he ate honey although the king had decreed all men should fast (see 1 Sam. 21:6; 14:24-27). Jesus showed the importance of wisdom and necessity. His disciples plucked grain and ate on the Sabbath. To change a lame man's ailments, Jesus healed on the Sabbath (see Mark 2:23; John 5:2-12). After Jairus' daughter's healing, Jesus asked her parents to give her something to eat (see Luke 8:56) because physical needs are important. One night at a prayer meeting, Holy Spirit showed me "B-12." The lady for whom I was praying later told me her doctor had said she needed to take B-12. She hadn't acted on his advice; because the Lord spoke it again through me, she knew He was nudging her about this. God made bodies to use certain nutrients and vitamins, and sometimes you need to replace what's been depleted or what your diet doesn't provide.

Opinions differ about medicine, but taking it doesn't necessarily denote a lack of faith but a practicality. Each person should go to God about prescriptions, and that may change with each healing need. God heals in many ways, and one method is through doctors and God-given medical advancements and knowledge. Medicines can eradicate certain ailments or make you feel more comfortable as healing progresses. When God's ready for you to quit taking it, He'll let you know by how your body feels, doctors' orders, a surety in your spirit, or Holy Spirit's revelation. However, if God tells you not to take something, don't take it. Medicine sometimes makes a well person sick or creates problems later in life. Obedience is part of healing; wisdom and spiritual discernment are crucial components.

However, although doctors have their place, the Lord wants to be first. Like the man for whom Jesus prayed was looking down when Jesus was right in front of him, He's in front of you, too. Doctors shouldn't be the first help you seek, and God's jealous of sharing His role. God sent Elijah to King Ahaziah because after he'd fallen through the lattice of his second-story room, he sent a messenger to a Baal prophet to ask if he'd be okay. Because he sought healing knowledge from someone besides God, an angel told Elijah to ask him if he inquired of Baal because "there is no God in Israel" (2 Kings 1:2-3). That question is appropriate today. You have a powerful, healing God, so why try everything else then go to Him as an after-thought or last resort? His healing's perfect and doesn't create side-effects, cost anything, or risk physical addictions. Like Jesus told the blind man, you should *look up* from the beginning and seek Him.

In the wilderness, once again the Hebrews faced a life-and-death dilemma. Deadly snakes were biting and killing them. People entreated Moses for deliverance, so the Lord instructed him to make a serpent and put it on a pole. Those bitten could look on that serpent and live (see Num. 21:8-9). This blind man looked up to where healing lived because "as Moses lifted up the serpent in the wilderness, even so must the Son of Man be lifted up" (John 3:14). Jesus proclaimed, "When you lift up the Son of Man, then you will know that I am He, and that I do nothing of Myself; but as My Father taught Me, I speak these things" (John 8:28). You lift up Jesus and look into His face because He has the Father's orders about your healing. Those who looked at the snake couldn't also look at their symptoms, so turning your eyes on Him moves your focus off your problems. You neglect healing, your own sight, by focusing elsewhere and not on the Lord.

Prophetic Actions

Another healing principle from this story is that Jesus usually heals in strange ways. His healings occurred as He operated the Father's way, despite how others perceived it. He often used prophetic actions, God's specific way to bring about healing. Prophetic actions require doing something as Holy Spirit reveals how He wants healing accomplished. My mother called those revelations God's M.O., that *method of operation* which brought the answer. One amazing miracle happened to me as a result of a prophetic action. I'd suffered several days with severe foot pain later diagnosed as gout. A friend felt led to wash my feet. By the next morning, my ankles and feet were nearly well! We've witnessed many miracles brought about by prophetic actions, which depend upon obedience. As a receiver of revelation, your responsibility is to share how God wants to accomplish the healing. Then the person needing healing also must act on Holy Spirit's directive. When he/she obeys, the healing circle is completed. Everyone must do his/her part.

I've seen many actions that looked silly but which touched the heavenlies—slamming a door, taking daily communion, breaking imaginary chains. Prophetic actions could range from anointing a prayer cloth to twirling around, but God-authored actions are powerful and productive. Massive examples permeate Scripture. Although Naaman had his own idea of how to be healed, God told him to dip in the Jordan (see 2 Kings 5); Moses stretched his rod over the Red Sea (see Exod. 14:26-27); Joshua marched around Jericho as God prescribed (see Josh. 6). Jesus healed through prophetic actions so often, this section could go in nearly every chapter of this book. He did "foolish" prophetic actions that seemed laughable but brought results. For this healing, Jesus spat on the blind man's eyes. Once, He told a man to stretch out his hand while another time He spat on a man's tongue (see Matt 12:13; Mark 7:33). After prophetic actions are revealed and acted upon, amazing events occur, even from things as foolish as spitting.

Awesome prophetic action results occurred when I preached in Italy. Riding on the plane that morning from Ireland, God spoke into my heart and sleep-deprived mind that I needed to change that night's sermon and instead preach about "Breakthrough." I'd gone to Europe with my sermons folder plump and ready; but none were about that subject. I spent the day with the Lord downloading into me. I felt led to do a prophetic action and burst balloons to signal breakthrough. If I'd been in the U.S., I could've run to Wal-Mart and bought them; in Italy I didn't have a car even if I knew where to go. A foreign country created no problem for the Lord, though. That night, a lady across the aisle had three balloons on the pew beside her! I somehow asked her in my non-existent Italian if I could have them. After she understood, she readily complied. As those balloons burst—first, then second, then third—each pop represented needed breakthrough. The anointing powerfully erupted that night. His ways are different from yours; if you want healings, miracles, or breakthroughs, you must do it *His* way. Prophetic actions may sound ludicrous; but oh, what amazing results occur!

Servanthood's Work

The Bible speaks often about workers, laborers, or helpers. Miracles and healings are performed as a result of serving others. You can show servanthood in many ways—helping build the church wing, babysitting for a new mother, cleaning the house for someone who had surgery. A servant must be a giver; show love to others; and "must not quarrel but be gentle to all, able to teach, patient, in humility correcting those who are in opposition" (2 Tim. 2:24-25). Jesus embodied servanthood in all aspects of His ministry. I love this scripture about His servanthood: "For He healed many, so that as many as had afflictions pressed about Him to touch Him" (Mark 3:10). The Greek word used here for *healed* is *therapeuo*, "to wait upon menially, to adore (God)...cure, heal, worship."[2] This word originally meant for one to accomplish lowly tasks as a domestic but later had a medical meaning because domestics' duties included caring for the sick. It evolved to indicate healing.[3] Like any job you're tapped to do, Jesus' job was to take care of the sick as He healed. You're a servant whether doing dishes or speaking healing to others.

As a servant to *all*, Jesus healed and delivered day or night— at church, in town, in the synagogue, by the sea, in the countryside. Healing also comes at varied times for and through you—at a home prayer meeting, at a casual encounter in the grocery store, in a church prayer line, on Facebook. As people approach for healing, you're a servant, even using your gifts. Once, Jesus left Galilee and went to Judea (see Matt. 19:1-2). He didn't have a dynamic revival planned; but great multitudes followed Him, and He healed as their servant. Even during His Gethsemane arrest, He healed. All Gospels tell the same story about how one of Jesus' friends cut off the ear of a man arresting Him (see Matt.

26:51; Mark 14:47; Luke 22:50; John 18:10). John identifies this disciple as Peter, who responded to the impending arrest in his typically rash way. He also names the man whose ear Peter cut off as Malchius, servant to the high priest (see John 18:10). Peter's attempt to show support of Jesus didn't impress the Master. He didn't view Peter's actions as justice or sticking up for a Friend but rather admonished him that their strength didn't lie in swords. Luke added a detail the others didn't. Jesus touched Malchius' ear and healed him (see Luke 22:51). Jesus' touch healed the blind man and others who were desperate, yet His touch healed even those considered His enemies. Even someone arresting Him with a murderous intention.

Part of servanthood is being aware of others' healing needs while protecting their dignity. Jesus was often deluged by requests from multitudes for miracles and healings, yet He cared about each individual and his/her dignity and privacy. For the blind man, before Jesus healed him, He led him out of town (see Mark 8:23). Scripture doesn't clarify why He took him there, but many possible reasons could necessitate separating some people from others. I think this time, an element of self-respect could've prompted the request. Another time when delivering a young man from demonic possession, Jesus showed His utter love for the young man. Because He saw others coming around, He healed the boy right then (see Mark 9:25). The Son of Man came to serve (see Mark 10:45), and He isn't in the embarrassment business. This blind man or the young man with demonic manifestations didn't need to be the object of pointing and whispering.

Jesus made one last request of the blind man: Don't go into town or tell anyone. He asked that often after healings. Many reasons may also have prompted this request. One could have been because of His servant character of humility. He understood that every ability comes from God; He didn't need accolades, nor should you. Making a name for yourself is a dangerous motivation that ultimately leads to downfall. I cringe when I hear ministers boast about healings they've performed as if humans could heal anyone of anything on their own. Jesus didn't heal to show His might and power, though He had massive numbers of healings about which He could've boasted. Instead, He said, "whoever desires to become great among you, let him be your servant" (Matt. 20:26). Jesus healed *all* because of obedience to God, compassion, and a servant's character, not with any other agenda. His using you to appropriate healing is about serving Him and others, not about you.

Conclusion

Before I was born, my parents became believers as a result of a healing. After my grandfather witnessed miracles by a faith healer in Hamilton, Ohio, and heard his words about Jesus' sacrifice and healing character, hope burned into Grandpa's broken heart. He'd been told his seventeen-year-old daughter wouldn't live to celebrate Christmas because of rheumatic heart disease. That night in Hamilton, not only did my grandfather give *his* heart to God, but he decided to give his daughter's ailing heart to the Lord. When he made plans to take her for prayer, his other children were mortified. Their sister was in such bad shape, she couldn't get up from bed except for limited walks in the house. Despite their objections, though, my grandfather was determined she'd make that hour's drive on those windy, bumpy roads. By that time, the revival had been moved into a tent on the outskirts of town. Crudely sawn boards perched atop tree stumps. Sawdust covered the grass, brown from the trampling feet of hopeful attendees. In those less-than-pristine circumstances, my grandpa found her healing as the preacher laid hands on her. She grew progressively better until she was well enough to get a job and drive an hour each way to Cincinnati to work. She celebrated that Christmas and more than fifty after that—long enough to meet her great-grandchildren.

Though miracles and healings are different, they both conquer needs in your body. As you take your eyes off what the world can do and go instead to God, He has healings and miracles not only for you but also through you for others. Like a great part of Jesus' job was to heal, serving others is part of your job description, too. Today, some of you need a dire healing. Though you may not have experienced the touch of great healing evangelists like A.A. Allen, William Branham, or Benny Hinn, Jesus' touch is still available. Malachi says "to you who fear My name the Sun of Righteousness shall arise with healing in His wings; and you shall go out and grow fat like stall-fed calves" (Mal. 4:2). I love that description, especially because it's a prophetic word about Jesus, the Healer. He arose and brought your healing. You grow fat with His blessings as healing comes in His wings, in whatever manner He chooses.

Questions to Ponder

Answers in the Appendix

1   a.   How is the story of the blind man at Bethsaida different from most of Jesus' healings?

     b.   Explain the difference between a miracle and a healing.

     c.   How does this story demonstrate a healing rather than a miracle?

     d.   How does a seed's growth reflect the process of healing?

2   a.   Explain an illness versus a symptom.

     b.   How do symptoms hinder healing?

     c.   Fill in the blanks: ___ the devil's ___ because ___ can ___ God's purpose.

3   a.   How do intercessors help in healing?

     b.   Give examples of when Jesus touched others for healing.

     c.   Explain how laying on of hands initiates healing.

     d.   How does Jesus touch others now for healing? Can you share a personal story?

4   a.   How should you be wise about your body?

     b.   Give biblical examples of people using wisdom about their bodies.

     c.   Does taking medicine or going to doctors always show a lack of faith?

     d.   How do Jesus' words to the blind man give instruction about whom you first approach for healing?

     e.   How does the story of Ahaziah also show this?

5   a.   What are prophetic actions?

b.   Give two examples from the author's life.

c.   Give two from Bible stories, including Jesus'. Do you have examples from your own life?

6   a.   Besides healing, how else can you demonstrate servanthood?

    b.   Explain how the evolution of the word *therapeuo* came to include healing.

    c.   How is Jesus your servanthood example?

    d.   Tell the story of how Jesus was a servant even while being arrested.

    e.   While healing their bodies, how did Jesus protect others' dignity?

    f.   What character trait defines Jesus?

DISCUSSION: Which principle from the story of the Bethsaida blind man or the healing of Malchius speaks most to you?

Chapter Two

The Finished Work

THAT NIGHT BENEATH THE TENT DIDN'T BRING A MIRACLE FOR MY aunt; but the healing eventually manifested because my grandfather heard of the finished work, believed, spoke, and activated faith by taking his daughter for prayer. That event accomplished so much more than her healing, though. My mom, dad, and other family members were brought into the Kingdom knowing the reality of what the Lord could do. My mom, especially, had many experiences that resulted in healings for our family. Once, when my younger brother Phillip had seizures, my parents believed the Lord would heal him. Then, one night when Mom was in bed, an angel entered the room. He opened a dresser drawer and asked if she wanted to put something into it.

"I can't," she responded. "It's already full."

"Exactly," the angel told her. "Jesus died for Phillip's healing. There's room for nothing else but his healing." Then the angel left. My brother is now in his sixties and has never suffered another seizure. That night from a heavenly emissary, my mom learned the message of Jesus' finished work for herself. It's done, so nothing but healing can fit into that place.

When something's finished, it's finished. The dishes, the antique you're redoing, the new recipe you're making for dinner, the marathon you're running. Each day you accomplish necessary chores by going through required steps. Every stage of the process is important for arriving at completion; but when the job's finished, it's finished. You understand this concept in daily life; the same principles apply to healing. Jesus paid the price once and for all for salvation, but that ransom also included healing. Because of His sacrificial act, it's a done deal. Nothing but your healing will fit there. Like you complete a project, speech, report, or laundry, your healing is also finished.

What Did Jesus Do?

One day, Jesus taught at a house among Pharisees and teachers from Galilee, Judea, and Jerusalem (see Mark 2:1-12; Luke 5:17-26), and "the power of the Lord was present to heal them" (Luke 5:17). However, such a crowd had gathered that many were unable to enter the house where He was teaching. Men attempted to bring in a bedridden, paralyzed man to set before Jesus, but they couldn't get through the crowd. Not willing to abandon hope, four men (in Mark 2:3) climbed to the housetop and let him and his bed down through the roof. Jesus saw their faith and proclaimed to the paralytic, "Man, your sins are forgiven you" (Luke 5:20). Jesus made this same bold statement in Matthew, which omitted the detail of lowering the man through the roof (see Matt. 9:2-7). After Jesus uttered this, some scribes were appalled that He spoke such blasphemy, which implied He could forgive this man's sins when God alone could do that.

However, Jesus knew their thoughts and asked if saying, "Your sins are forgiven you" or "Arise and walk" (Matt. 9:5) was easier. He then told them He had power to forgive sin. He turned to the sick man and demonstrated His healing power by saying, "arise, take up your bed, and go to your house" (Luke 5:24). The man immediately got up, took up his bed, returned to his house, and praised God for his healing. Everyone was amazed and glorified God but were also fearful and commented on the strange things they'd seen.

He Did It All

In this story Jesus made a connection between forgiveness from sin and healing because of His finished work. His saying the man's sins were forgiven was controversial; but He asked which is easier, forgiving sins or healing. That statement links removal of sin and healing of sickness. When you're saved, you're also healed because He died not only for salvation but for your healing, too. Other Jesus stories make a connection between them. Once, after a disreputable woman had washed His feet, Jesus told her that her faith had saved her (see Luke 7:50). This word for *saved* is *sozo,* which lists several definitions, including "to save, i.e. deliver...heal...be (make) whole."[1] When you're *sozoed,* He saves, heals, delivers, and makes you whole in spirit, soul, and body. As He pronounced both salvation and healing for this man, He put them into the same category. Like you accept salvation by faith, you also accept healing by faith.

In another story Jesus links the two. On His way to Jerusalem, He passed through Samaria and Galilee. In a village, he was met by ten lepers, who called out for healing mercy. Because they were considered unclean, they stood a distance away (see Luke 17:11-19). Observing Jewish law, He instructed them to go to the priest. On their way they were healed as they obeyed. However, only one of the lepers came back to thank Him. That man who returned was referred to as a Samaritan, and Jesus called him a foreigner. The implication is that the rest were most likely Jews. Many believe this story is a parable about how Jews rejected Him while Gentiles appreciated Him. However, another interpretation exists. When Jesus asked where the others were who should have also given God glory, He said, "Arise, go your way. Your faith has made you well" (Luke 17:19). One translation could be, "Your faith has saved you."[2] By His coming back, the Samaritan leper was saved while the others weren't. This man received the dual blessing of healing *and* salvation, which the unappreciative lepers squandered. Using the same wording for both healing and salvation again links them.

David admonishes not to "forget...His benefits: who forgives all your iniquities, who heals all your diseases" (Ps. 103:2-3). I love that not only does David mention sins and diseases together, but he uses the word "benefits." When you come to Him, He gives you a benefits package; and both are included, as well as much more! Paul connects them by saying God wishes you to "prosper in all things and be in health, just as your soul prospers" (3 John 2). God desires prosperity in every area of your life—spirit, soul, and body. Paul also prayed that your "whole spirit, soul, and body be preserved" (1 Thess. 5:23), thus putting the body and spirit into the same category. He says by Jesus' sacrifice, "you were bought at a price; therefore [you should] glorify God in your body and in your spirit" (1 Cor. 6:20). He died for your sins, so His sacrifice should be apparent in your spirit and manifested in your healthy body (see 2 Cor. 4:11). With the declaration of faith that Jesus is Lord for salvation, healing is yours, too. Jesus told His disciples, "Behold, I cast out demons and perform cures today and tomorrow, and the third day I shall be perfected [resurrected]" (Luke 13:32). The words *cures* and *heal* (translation used in Acts 4:30) are *iasis,* meaning deliverance, healing, and salvation.[3] Salvation and healing—they're part of the same package.

It's Finished

Early in His ministry, Jesus told disciples His job was to do the Father's will and "to finish His work" (John 4:34). That work was completed when God gave His Son to come to earth, die, and rise again for you to have eternal life and the gift of Holy Spirit. He suffered greatly on His way to the cross. He'd been denied and betrayed by those He loved. He was ridiculed, taunted, and scorned. The scourging that created His stripes was so bad it nearly killed Him *before* His crucifixion (see Matt. 27:26). Then He died on the cross. Nobody forced Him to take stripes or give His life; He willingly did it because He and His Father love you (see John 10:18). He could have given up after the first betrayal or painful lash, but He chose instead to go the distance. Those bloody lashes on His back and nail-pierced hands paid for salvation and healing. Isaiah prophesied that Messiah would be "wounded for our transgressions... bruised for our iniquities; the chastisement for our peace was upon Him, and by His stripes we *are* healed" (Isa. 53:5). Within this same sentence, we're assured that Jesus' broken body was the answer to our sins; plus, His stripes healed us—mentally ("our peace") and physically.

Peter quoted Isaiah but changed the verb tense from *are* to *were*. Jesus "who Himself bore our sins in His own body on the tree, that we, having died to sins, might live for righteousness—by whose stripes you *were* healed" (see 1 Pet. 2:24). You were saved and healed, so you can now live victoriously in Jesus' righteousness. It's finished. Jesus punctuated the idea of the finished work when He gave disciples promises also in past tense—"believe that you have received it, and it will be yours" (Mark 11:24 NIV). He said to the centurion, "as you have believed, so let it be done for you" (Matt. 8:13). Because *have received* and *have believed* are in the past, the implication is you must first believe healing was already accomplished; then you'll see results. Symptoms may still exist and evidence of the miracle not yet come, but you should believe you've received healing because it's Christ's finished work. If you know His sacrifice paid the price long ago, you can claim your healing. It's finished, and Jesus doesn't have to go back to the whipping post.

Even before His horrific, impending ordeal, Jesus prayed, "I have glorified You on the earth. I have finished the work which You have given Me to do" (John 17:4). *Finished* is *teleioo*, "to complete...accomplish... consummate...(make) perfect."[4] Before the hard part of the scourging and the cross, He'd accomplished what He needed to do while on earth. He'd healed, taught, loved, formed relationships, walked with and mentored disciples. However, His sacrifice, which would save and heal after He was gone, was yet to occur. He again used *finished* while on the cross but with a slightly different word and connotation. As He hung dying, His last words, "It is finished!" (John 19:30) used *teleo*, similar yet different from the first usage. In addition to some of the other definitions, *teleo* also means to "execute, conclude, discharge (a debt)...make an end, expire...pay."[5] His final purpose for coming to earth was completed.

Another aspect of *teleo* is that the Greek tense means it's been done permanently with continuous results.[6] That proclamation of "It is finished" as He laboriously sucked in His last, precious breath, forever discharged man's debt and gave salvation and healing through this ultimate ordeal. The price He paid for salvation and healing was His death, which concluded the law of sin and death into which man was born. He ended the work as He became your sin put to death, thus paying that debt He didn't owe and which you couldn't pay. I once heard the analogy that it's like you used your credit card to accumulate debt, but He paid the bill when it came due. His finished work was a wondrous package you can grasp by faith—salvation, healing, and Holy Spirit.

Atonement

His work was finished as He took your place to substitute for your sin. That's atonement. God made earth and intended for man to abide with Him. Adam's sin made that impossible, so man was doomed to live under curses—poverty, sorrow, toil, trials, murder, death, rivalries (see Gen. 3). Part of the curse was also sin and sickness. Because of Adam's sin, God required men to bring a blood sacrifice periodically to substitute for their transgressions. A story demonstrating this concept is when people had sinned during the wilderness journey, so God released a plague. Moses told Aaron to put fire from the altar and incense into a censer and take it among the people to make atonement, appease God's wrath, and turn the plague aside. As Aaron ran among them, he was their substitute; that replacement turned the penalty away from them. They lived, and the plague stopped (see Num. 16:46-50). That's how atonement works.

A beautiful parallel of Christ's substitution is the story of Abraham and Isaac. When God asked Abraham to sacrifice his "only son" (Gen. 22:2), that Hebrew word was *yachid*—"an only one, an only child, a precious life."[7] Although Abraham dearly loved Isaac, he obeyed and laid his son on the altar. Then God provided a ram in the bush for Abraham to sacrifice instead of Isaac. That's when Abraham knew God as Jehovah Jireh, "The-Lord-Will-Provide" (Gen. 22:13-14). The blood of Abraham's ram covered sin temporarily before he had to sacrifice again. However, when God put another Ram in the thicket—Jesus, *His* own beloved *Yachid*—sacrificing didn't need to occur regularly because He made a once-and-for-all atonement through God's only Son's sacrifice (see John 3:16). When someone substitutes for another, he replaces that person and suffers for him/her. Jesus became sin, substituted, and suffered that Calvary trip to bear your sins and sicknesses once and for all (see 2 Cor. 5:21).

Paul said if God is for you, no one or nothing else can be against you (see Rom. 8:31). God proved that by giving His *Yachid*, and Jesus proved it by His willing sacrifice while you were a sinner. His substitution was prophesied by many. Job's friend said you'd be delivered "from going down to the Pit; [for God] found a ransom" (Job 33:24-25). Matthew 8:17 quotes Isaiah's prophetic word: "Surely He has borne our griefs and carried our sorrows" (Isa. 53:4). The Hebrew words for *griefs* and *sorrows* both mean "sicknesses, both spiritual and physical."[8] On that cross as

He bore your sins (spiritual), He also carried your sicknesses (physical). Using *has borne* indicates that as a substitute, He transported it away.

Paul also said, "He who did not spare His own Son, but delivered Him up for us all, how shall He not with Him also freely give us all things?" (Rom. 8:32). Think of that! God loved us greatly, even while we were sinners (see Rom. 5:8). His priceless gift of His Son was the ultimate sacrifice, so why would He limit Jesus' purpose to salvation but withhold healing? He'll "supply *all* your need according to His riches in glory by Christ Jesus" (Phil. 4:19). All things from your rich Father include a lot—deliverance, healing, salvation, and whatever else you need. The Father and Son's sacrifice covered everything. Why would you lack when God's character is to provide all your needs, and His most precious Gift paid the price? It's finished.

The "first man Adam became a living being. The last Adam became a life-giving spirit" (1 Cor. 15:45). While the first Adam brought sin and death to the world, this last Adam brought life—spiritually and physically—as He bore all things to the cross. Paul explains how Jesus changed Adam's curse:

> *Through one man sin entered the world, and death through sin, and thus death spread to all men.... Death reigned from Adam to Moses, even over those who had not sinned according to the likeness of the transgression of Adam, who is a type of Him who was to come. But...if by the one man's offense many died, much more the grace of God and the gift by the grace of the one Man, Jesus Christ, abounded to many* (Romans 5:12, 14-15).

The last Adam sacrificed, once and for all. If you don't recognize He's already completed it, you miss the purpose of His suffering and sacrifice. You're healed; now, claim it. Are you ignoring the power of His finished work?

Because we live in this world, curses run rampant. As the curse personified, He "redeemed us from the curse of the law, having become a curse for us" (Gal. 3:13). The Old Covenant brought blessings for obedience and curses for disobedience (see Deut. 28). Because He became the curse, now all we have left are the blessings. We're under grace, not Adam's curse (see Rom. 6:14). When Paul suffered hardships for Jesus, He told Paul His "grace is sufficient" (2 Cor. 12:9). That includes whatever plagues you—illnesses, generational curses, emotional issues, financial woes, thorns in the flesh—*all things*. Grace took Him to the cross, and grace is your sufficiency. He came to "reconcile [you]...through the cross, thereby putting to death the enmity [of the law]" (Eph. 2:16). As you bring your needs to Him in faith, salvation and healing belong to you because He constantly makes intercession for you through Holy Spirit (see Heb. 7:25).

Power in the House

This event teaches much about Jesus' healing ministry and how to receive His finished work. Luke says a healing presence was mighty in that packed house. This tells me that when God's presence enters a room, a great anointing exists. I've experienced multiple healings and miracles as the Lord's power entered, so thick it had substance. The crowd's reaction to this miracle is typical of Jesus' healings. People were amazed and frightened because they'd never seen anything like it (see Mark 2:12). That's a response even seasoned believers exhibit as Holy Spirit's power permeates the atmosphere to bring signs and wonders. People who see them are in awe.

Jesus performed a miracle after coming from Judea and a nobleman came from Capernaum. Though the man had a high, royal position, he'd heard of Jesus and sought Him to heal his ill son, who was near death (see John 4:46-54). After he approached, Jesus responded, "Unless you people see signs and wonders, you will by no means believe" (John 4:48).

After the son was healed, the nobleman and his entire household became believers. Even those who spread clothes (in Mark 11:8) and palm leaves on His triumphal return were there because of the miracle of Lazarus' resurrection (see John 12:18). Signs and wonders have a greater purpose than just to heal. That anointing accomplishes miracles, which draw the lost. When people witness that, they're changed. Large numbers followed Jesus because of His power, but He was always aware of the lost and bringing them to Him.

One Saturday morning with uncombed hair and dressed in my old bathrobe, I was doing devotions on my porch so I could enjoy the bright, eastern sun. I'd opened my Bible when I felt led to pray for a lady in the hospital. As I did, I saw a vision of sharp, white lines on a heart monitor. As that vision grew more vivid, I knew I should go pray for her right then; but I came up with excuses. Saturday was my cleaning day, and my house was beyond the bad point. I had a deep stack of overdue papers awaiting my red pen. I'd thought all week I might take a nap. I sat a couple minutes thinking of a plethora of reasons *not* to go but knew I had one good reason I should—because He said so. I gathered my Bible, went into the house, and told my husband I felt an urgency to visit her. We dressed quickly and headed out. In the ICU, she was attached to a heart monitor and gasping for air through breathing tubes. Looking grim, her sister and daughter were beside her bed, devastated by the doctor's words that she was dying. Wade and I anointed her, laid hands on her, and prayed. Like Jesus in that over-crowded house, I felt power in that room and knew He'd done a work. Vital signs immediately improved. Her wheezing stopped, and she began talking. Before we left, she asked us to go to Frisch's to get her a fish sandwich. That event spoke volumes to her family members. His presence has a purpose and power.

Perseverance

Another principle from this story is that perseverance to grab the finished work is rewarded. Not only the paralytic but others had come for the Master's touch. As they crowded into that house, they were wall to wall, pressed against one another, smelling odors of those around. Tempers may have flared in the congestion of those straining to experience Jesus. Yet, they persisted and stayed. Though this story tells about only one miracle, surely others with desperate needs were healed that day when they came to Jesus. At times healing requires standing and waiting until the Master passes by. Other times, though, you must do more than settle in. You must press in actively toward Him. Scripture doesn't say this man's friends sought healing for themselves because often it's about others, not you. That may take you outside your comfort zone, but going to your usual place in the Lord hasn't brought your answers. As you diligently seek Him, you remove the roof from your expectations, and He takes you higher. He responds as pressing in puts action to your faith.

One Sunday morning at church, the Lord gave me a word of knowledge that He was going to heal someone who had cancer. Before anyone could respond, however, the church's pastor erroneously applied an interpretation to that revelation and prayed a generic prayer. I cringed inside but observed godly order and didn't correct the pastor although I knew what the Lord had spoken to me. Herb, a prolific operator in words of knowledge himself, also knew it was correct. After church, Wade and I were sitting down for lunch at his mother's house when Herb drove up, wanting to claim that miracle. Doctors had told him the growth on his face was cancer. Wade, his mother, and I prayed for him and claimed the healing Holy Spirit had revealed. The next week before church, as he entered, Herb's eyes swept the room until he spotted us in front. He hustled down, his smile bigger than his normal toothy grin. He turned his cheek toward us and ran his hand over clean, smooth skin where the ugly growth had been. It had begun to dry up after we prayed and had fallen off later in the week. By his perseverance and courage to drive to Wade's mother's house and believe for something big, Herb had taken the roof off his expectations and actively sought his miracle. God responded.

Perseverance means you push in despite obstacles. For some that means you press past massive crowds so you can touch His robe. For others, it may be not giving up until the Lord delivers your heathen, possessed daughter. Sometimes you should appropriate your or others' healing by taking the roof off and going into the crowded house. What if Hannah had given up instead of persevering to birth Israel's greatest priest, prophet, and judge? What if Joshua had abandoned his orders before the seventh time on the seventh day around Jericho? Perseverance says don't give up, because that miracle may be just beyond the roof of your expectations.

Holy Spirit's Arrival

Jesus' finished work was accomplished by His death, resurrection, ascension, and arrival of Holy Spirit. He promised that,

> *He who believes in Me, the works that I do he will do also; and greater works than these he will do, because I go to My Father. And whatever you ask in My name, that I will do, that the Father may be glorified in the Son* (John 14:12-13).

We can do these things *because* He went to the Father, and that event preceded Holy Spirit's arrival to give us power. As John baptized Him, Holy Spirit rested upon Jesus as a dove, and He was filled with the Spirit (see Luke 3:22). Holy Spirit guided Jesus' ministry; now, He guides ours. Like Holy Spirit infilled Jesus, that unlimited power operates through us. When people look at your life, do they see those greater works? Unfortunately, many believers don't do greater works because they do *no* works of Holy Spirit. Most churches are satisfied to practice impotent religion. They don't desire, let alone seek, power in their midst even though that power can bring wonderful, necessary results.

Before He left, Jesus told of the Spirit's necessity: "It is to your advantage that I go away; for if I do not go away, the Helper will not come to you; but if I depart, I will send Him to you" (John 16:7). That word translated here as *advantage* is *sumphero*, to "be better for...be expedient (for), be good."[9] This same word is used as *profitable* in Acts 20:20. His life's sacrifice and finished work was for your profit. Whatever's profitable is to your advantage, and that's why Jesus died. The King James Version uses a different word for *advantage—expedient*. I like that word. It implies tremendous importance for Jesus to leave and Holy Spirit to arrive. He gave His life for your profit. Holy Spirit and healing are part of that.

When He died, arose, then ascended, His work was finished, but people's needs weren't diminished. Therefore, Holy Spirit allows you to do the greater works Jesus foretold. Spirit-filled believers are directed by Him as He reveals secrets, teaches them to pray, and leads them in that prayer because He knows how to pray when they don't. That's accomplished through His language and revelation gifts (see 1 Cor. 12:8-10), which I'll describe further in another chapter. This level of walking in Holy Spirit is different from His dwelling in you as a result of salvation. Being filled with the Spirit, or baptized in the Spirit with evidence of speaking in tongues, gives access to His nine gifts as overcoming weapons that can conquer everything, including sickness. He works through those gifts activated in Spirit-filled believers.

Holy Spirit and Angels

As part of Jesus' finished work, Holy Spirit accomplishes much for and through you as He partners with angels to send them on assignment to help you or give them charge over you (see Ps. 91:11). Angels are so common Paul advises you to be kind to strangers because you may have "unwittingly entertained angels" (Heb. 13:2). He clarifies their roles by saying, they're "sent forth to minister for those who will inherit salvation" (Heb. 1:14). That statement tells me if Christians are already inheriting salvation, angels come to minister to other needs, such as healing. Paul connects angels and Holy Spirit when he first mentions them then says you can't neglect your salvation (and the healing that accompanies it) because it was of spoken by Jesus, attested to by His followers, confirmed by signs and wonders, and demonstrated by His gifts (see Heb. 2:3-4). Angels' ministry in conjunction with Holy Spirit accomplishes much.

Angels were part of Jesus' life experiences and ministry. When Joseph discovered Mary was pregnant and debated about what action to pursue, an angel came in a dream to assure him the Baby she'd conceived was from Holy Spirit. Before His birth, God sent the angel Gabriel to tell Mary of His plan. An angel appeared to shepherds and announced His birth; then hosts of angels proclaimed the birth (see Matt. 1:20; Luke 1:26-27; 2:9, 13). Angels ministered to and strengthened Jesus during His wilderness journey and when He prayed in Gethsemane (see Mark 1:13; Luke 22:43). He clarified that twelve legions of angels were at His beck and call during His arrest. An angel rolled the stone away after His resurrection, then proclaimed He'd risen (see Matt. 26:53; 28:2; Luke 24:6).

One story about Jesus involves angels and healing. A great multitude made up of the sick, blind, lame, and paralyzed had gathered at the Pool of Bethesda (see John 5:2-9). Periodically, an angel stirred up the water, and whoever rushed in first would be healed. Then, the Healer Himself showed up. As Jesus arrived that day, one man lying there had been sick thirty-eight years and had come often to the pool. However, because he was so ill and didn't have help, he was unable to get into the water. Each time he was ready to step in, someone pressed in front of him. Does that sound familiar? No matter how you try, something happens to keep you from receiving—fear from a bad doctor's report, inadequate finances, other people's inconsiderate actions. Can you imagine the pushing and shoving that occurred as the sick, desperate for God's miracle, approached their only hope? Then, that day, Hope Himself came walking by.

Jesus saw the man and asked, "Do you want to be made well?" (John 5:6). The man had faith enough to stand by that pool for all those years, but his answer showed his lack of faith in and understanding of Jesus as the Healer whom the pool represented. As Jesus asked about his healing, he uttered why he *couldn't* be healed—he didn't have anyone to put him into the water (see John 5:6-7). That's like us. Instead of trusting Jesus, we make excuses for why we can't be healed or believe in something else besides the Lord. However, Jesus didn't scold him for his lack of faith. He simply said, "Rise, take up your bed and walk" (John 5:8). That symbol of his ailment had carried him all those years, but now he was to carry it as a symbol of Jesus' healing authority. As he obeyed, he was immediately healed. Your ailment may have hung on long—nearly four decades for this man. You may have given up or rehearsed reasons why you're not healed. Oh, but, things change when Jesus comes by.

This Bethesda story shows how Holy Spirit works with angels to bring about greater works. During our services, Wade, others, and I have many revelations, especially words of knowledge, which result in miracles. I liken those revelations to the angel stirring the waters. Although God's in the healing business all the time, when Holy Spirit spotlights something specific, a healing anointing for that ailment comes into our midst. After a word of knowledge is received—about anything from family strife to dire physical problems—that need is healed because of the revelation. I believe right then an angel is present with an anointing to heal that particular issue. That angel stirs up those miracle waters for healing to those who respond.

Some ministries experience regular miracles/healings for specific maladies because angels bring that anointing into their midst. Many times, we've interceded for pregnancies, including for two of Wade's daughters who had problems with conception. After God gave me a *rhema* about how to stand in the gap for them, they both became pregnant. They delivered their babies the same night, and one had twins. One story I love happened overseas. After I'd spoken at a church in Italy, a mother came forward and told me through an interpreter that her daughter was having trouble conceiving. I prayed and felt anointing flow. I didn't think any more about it until the next year. Wade and I returned to Italy and spoke at that same church. After I preached that night, I recognized that mother as she hustled down to tell me something through the interpreter. She was excited but became frustrated by the language barrier. She finally turned and motioned to someone in the back. Down the aisle came a young woman, her daughter, pushing a baby carriage.

In other biblical examples of angelic intervention, God sent angels to humans for a reason and still does. Elisha had angels as helpers in battle. An angel followed the children at the Red Sea and covered them with a cloud, which allowed them to be hidden and escape from the Egyptians. God sent an angel before Abraham's servant to prepare the way to take Rebekah back as Isaac's wife (see 2 Kings 6:17-20; Exod. 14:19; Gen. 24:7). An angel ministered to Elijah, and he was directed by an angel (see 1 Kings 19:5; 2 Kings 1:15). God still uses angels for specific reasons. At times when I've felt angels present, I've dispatched them into situations to do a work (see Ps. 103:20) and have seen wondrous results. Often, like at the Pool of Bethesda, they come for healing. Sometimes, like with Zacharias, they bring important information (see Luke 1:11). They take people home to Jesus or rescue from an impending accident as they steer the car from danger. They put protection over your kids when you can't get to them.

Years ago, Marjorie longed for more than she'd experienced at her powerless church. During that decade of faith healers, stories penetrated her heart, especially their description of being filled with Holy Spirit and speaking another language. Her search for a Spirit-filled assembly led her to a local church's basement where others hungry for a deeper walk had gathered while they built their own church. One night at a revival meeting, Marjorie felt something (an angel) engulf her so strongly she could barely stay seated. She left wanting more; the next day, she eagerly counted the minutes until service time. Then, she and her skeptical husband loaded up the kids. She wasn't disappointed as an angelic presence again surrounded her. After witnessing her growing fervor, her husband leaned over and whispered, "If ya dance like them people, I'll drag ya outa here by the haira yer head." She sat quietly, feeling as if she'd burst.

Shortly, a soft-spoken lady in a shirt-waist dress and a bun perched atop her head turned and murmured, "Honey, if ya don't do what the Lord's telling ya, ya'll regret it the resta yer life." That was all Marjorie needed. She began to dance, or shout, as we Pentecostals call it. As fast as her gyrating feet allowed, she danced while blubbering loudly in tongues. Unfortunately, her seat was close to a cast-iron stove; the narrow opening was difficult to squeeze through. As she danced, oblivious of her surroundings, her arm scraped that stove and cut a deep gash. Gushing blood told her she should stop for medical help, but she couldn't. Others rushed to her, but the pastor said to leave her alone because he saw an angel beside her. That heavenly emissary had come to that basement congregation to bring Marjorie a deeper walk that served her all her years. However, the angel also brought healing. As she shouted with abandon and blurted her new-found language, the gash on her arm healed, better than any ER doctor could've stitched her up. Angels have a purpose.

Your Role in Healing

His finished work left you with much to do. Your role is the same as first century disciples. When the resurrected Jesus told His disciples to "wait for the Promise of the Father" (Acts 1:4), He was referring to Holy Spirit. Isn't it amazing that Jesus mentioned Him as a precious Promise the Father would fulfill? A few verses later, He told them they'd "receive power when the Holy Spirit [came] upon [them]" (Acts 1:8). As a result, they witnessed about Him throughout the world and did many miraculous works after they were filled with the Spirit. Once, for example, Peter and John saw a forty-plus-year-old man who'd been born lame and was brought daily to beg at the temple gate, the Gate Beautiful. Peter took him by the hand and asked him to stand. As he complied, he received strength in his feet and ankle bones. Onlookers saw that miracle and were filled with wonder (see Acts 3:2-10). Another time, Peter was instrumental in healing a paralyzed man, bedridden eight years. As a result, two towns, Lydda and Sharon, were saved (see Acts 9:33-35). Philip did great miracles and deliverances that drew others (see Acts 8:5-8).

Once, a great crowd gathered in Jerusalem and brought the sick into the street to lay them on couches and beds so if Peter couldn't touch them, his shadow would fall across them. Another crowd from cities around Jerusalem also gathered, bringing those sick or possessed, and all were healed (see Acts 5:15-16). Through Peter, Tabitha was raised from the dead, and many were saved. When Paul resurrected Eutychus after his fall from a window, those present were greatly encouraged (see Acts 9:36-42; 20:9-12). Events wrought through disciples by Holy Spirit changed recipients' lives, those who witnessed it, and those God used for the miracle. As people saw signs and wonders, even those scared to join the disciples' ministry "esteemed them highly" (Acts 5:13); therefore, many got saved. If great men of God used Jesus' example and Holy Spirit's direction and power, why should you settle for less than miracles, deliverances, resurrections, and salvations? That should make you confident to step into your own role as He moves on you to perform signs and wonders through Holy Spirit's ability and to make a difference in the Kingdom and others' lives. Like first century disciples, your job is to bring the greater works He promised to your life and others'.

You should believe Jesus' words: "If I do not do the works of My Father, do not believe Me; but if I do, though you do not believe Me, believe the works, that you may know and believe that the Father is in Me, and I in Him" (John 10:37-38). Your job is to demonstrate the Father by doing what He does. Everything—even mighty works performed through you—is about His ability and your obedience, not about you or your ability. Although God used them mightily and others esteemed them highly, disciples kept their gifts in perspective. After people exalted Peter at the Gate Beautiful, he told them it wasn't by his power but God's. He also told Cornelius to stand up and not bow to him because he was just a man (Acts 3:12-13; 10:25-26). As you accomplish greater and sometimes impossible works, remember that it has nothing to do with your ability but everything to do with His. You can "be strong in the Lord and in the power of His might" (Eph. 6:10) but give the glory to Him.

Bringing healing and deliverance to those in need is demonstrated by the Good Samaritan. Samaritans were considered the lowest of society (see John 4:9). Religion's best, the Pharisees, avoided them. However, the Samaritan alone was willing to minister to the injured man's needs when religious people passed him by (see Luke 10:25-37). He didn't think of why he couldn't or shouldn't help but rather used his resources to appropriate healing for another. Religion often neglects one great Resource—Holy Spirit's healing power. Once, when Jesus was still walking with them, disciples asked how they could do the works of God. He told them that to do the work of God, "believe in Him whom He sent" (John 6:28-29). This means not only to believe in Jesus but also Holy Spirit.

Sin and Sickness

The finished work took both sin and sickness to the cross, so a definite connection exists between the two. One day, Jesus passed a man blind from birth (see John 9:1-34). He stopped, spat on the ground, made clay, and covered the blind man's eyes with the clay. Then He told him to wash in the Pool of Siloam. He obeyed Jesus and returned seeing. Disciples wondered whose sin had caused the blindness—his or his parents. People often erroneously judge others who need healing and say someone must've sinned or he/she wouldn't be sick. Like those in this story, many believe sickness comes because of your or your parents' sins. Actually, sickness is part of the curse Jesus freed you from, but many causes can still can affect you—what or how much you eat, sleep habits, improperly prepared foods, levels of activity, exposure to viruses. Some sicknesses come from toxins in workplaces, homes, or the atmosphere. Some result from behaviors such as substance abuse, unprotected sex, or many reasons.

Everything in your life works for your good (see Rom. 8:28), but that doesn't mean everything that comes into your life is good. God doesn't make you sick, because "Every good gift and every perfect gift is from above, and comes down from the Father" (James 1:17). Sickness isn't good, so it can't come from Him. However, sometimes you open a door to receive sickness, or He allows it for a bigger purpose. Jesus said sin didn't cause the man's blindness but the Father permitted it so His mighty works might be revealed through Jesus. For this situation, neither the blind man nor his parents had sinned and brought the curse. However, His saying sin didn't cause the blindness doesn't negate the biblical connection between sin and sickness. Paul linked them: "the law of the Spirit of life in Christ Jesus has made me free from the law of sin and death" (Rom. 8:2). Because of His sacrifice, you gained freedom as sin's curses were broken, but a correlation still exists between sin and receiving from God. The psalmist says, "No good thing will He withhold from those who walk uprightly" (Ps. 84:11).

The Hebrews were in Egypt when God struck Egyptians with plagues. Then, they left toward their Promised Land. After they'd passed through the Red Sea, God gave them a healing covenant, His first one with His wilderness children. God's addressing healing first on the journey tells me His children's physical well-being is high on His list of what He wants to give them. There at Marah, He revealed His character and redemptive name, Jehovah Rapha, the Healer (see Exod. 15:25-26). But He also gave Moses a command:

> *If you diligently heed the voice of the Lord your God and do what is right in His sight, give ear to His commandments and keep all His statutes, I will put none of the diseases on you which I have brought on the Egyptians. For I am the Lord who heals you (Exodus 15:26).*

He was the Healer who promised healing with one stipulation—*if.* *If* you heed the Lord's voice, do what's right, listen to and keep His commandments and statutes, He'll keep Egypt's plagues away from them. *If.*

Divine health comes with an *if.* Although nothing you can do earns the gift of grace (see Eph. 2:8-9), rewards come through obedience to God. Many scriptures connect healing or other blessings with obedience. David says, "The Lord has recompensed me according to my righteousness, according to the cleanness of my hands in His sight" (Ps. 18:24). Your receiving good things is commensurate with obedience to His law because obedience issues forth from the heart. Solomon says to, "Fear the Lord and depart from evil. It will be health to your flesh, and strength to your bones" (Prov. 3:7-8), and God doesn't prosper those who cover their sins (see Prov. 28:13). Isaiah says, "The Lord will strike Egypt, He will strike and heal it; they will return to the Lord, and He will be entreated by them and heal them" (Isa. 19:22). God can't look on sin (see Hab. 1:13), so it distances you from Him.

New Testament scriptures also connect sin and sickness. After healing the paralytic man, Jesus asked if it were easier to say, "Your sins are forgiven you" or "Arise and walk" (Matt. 9:5). After He healed the man at Bethesda, He later found him at the temple. Jesus admonished him to "Sin no more" so something worse wouldn't afflict him (John 5:14). That Greek word for *sin* is *hamartano*, "to miss the mark (and so not share in the prize)."[10] Your prize is healing, but sin keeps that from happening. Though He said the blindness wasn't the result of sin, this later comment shows a relationship. Paul gave a hard admonition to those who partake of communion unworthily: "He who eats and drinks in an unworthy manner eats and drinks judgment to himself...*For this reason* [sin] *many are weak and sick among you, and many sleep*" (1 Cor. 11:29-30). Many become sick and die as a result of sin. Each scripture shows a connection between receiving from God and obedience to His commandments.

James also makes a connection by saying that praying in faith saves the sick and brings forgiveness for his sins. He also instructs us to pray for each other in order to be healed (see James 5:15-16). That's clear—confessing your sin causes sickness to be healed. Ephesians connects long life and obeying the commandment to honoring parents (see Eph. 6:2-3). Long life and blessings connect with obedience to Him. Sin and sickness have a relationship. You should repent, claim your healing, then live to please Him. Seek the Kingdom of God and righteousness before anything; then everything will be given to you (see Matt. 6:33). That's His promise.

Conclusion

We once travelled to Tennessee to preach and visit friends. The night before we arrived, God spoke a message through a dream: "Expect more." I soon learned what that meant when in the afternoon we visited a lady with cancer. She'd been unable to walk because of radiation burns on her feet. She was resigned to experiencing horrific side effects; but when I gave her that message, illumination came on her face. Then Wade prayed repetitively, "Resurrection power." Those two communications from the Lord took root in her heart. She didn't have to suffer those things because His finished work had taken care of it. She claimed that finished work and was well enough to go to church that night.

Because Jesus was the ransom for sins and sicknesses, it's finished. When His work was finished, yours began. Your job is to bring that finished work into reality through Holy Spirit's power and persevere though your or another's body doesn't yet show the evidence. As healing power comes into your midst through angels, you can rest assured He has a healing for whosoever will. Many are hurting and need Holy Spirit's power that operates through you; if you neglect to help the sick, you neglect Jesus (see Matt. 25:43-44). After His resurrection, Jesus sent disciples to preach the gospel and then see signs and wonders (see Mark 16:15). Are you still doing that?

Questions to Ponder

Answers in the Appendix

1   a.   What does the statement mean that Jesus "did it all"?

     b.   Explain *sozo.*

     c.   Give lessons taught in the story of the ten lepers.

     d.   Choose two pieces of evidence that show the connection between salvation and healing.

2   a.   How was the finished work accomplished?

     b.   How does Peter's quote differ from Isaiah's and demonstrate the finished work?

     c.   Show how the difference between the Greek words *teleioo* and *teleo* expresses Christ's accomplishment in dying.

     d.   What does that mean for us?

3   a.   Explain atonement.

     b.   Choose either Aaron or Abraham and tell how their stories demonstrate atonement.

     c.   How is the story of Abraham like Jesus' sacrifice? How do they differ?

     d.   Fill in the blanks: God's ___ gift of His ___ was the ___ ___, so why would He limit Jesus' ___ to ___ but withhold ___?

     e.   Who are the first man Adam and the last man Adam?

     f.   What word best describes Jesus' sacrifice?

4   a.   What was the healing presence in the house?

     b.   What happens when that presence comes into a place?

     c.   How do people react to it?

d. How did the nobleman respond to his son's healing?

5 a. Explain perseverance for healing.

b. How does this story show perseverance?

c. Give other examples of how people pressed in until Jesus healed them. Give a time when you've received your answer through perseverance.

6 a. What part does Holy Spirit have in the greater works Jesus promised?

b. Jesus said it's to your advantage Holy Spirit comes. What are various translations of the word *advantage*?

c. Give ways Holy Spirit helps you.

d. What's the difference between receiving Holy Spirit through salvation and being *filled* with the Spirit?

7 a. How does Holy Spirit accomplish His will on earth?

b. Give two ways angels were significant in Jesus' life.

c. How long had the man at Bethesda been sick?

d. How did his answer to Jesus show lack of faith and under-standing?

e. Explain which Holy Spirit gift the author compares to the angel troubling the water?

f. Give reasons for angelic visits.

8 a. What's the "Promise of the Father"?

b. Give two miracles performed by first century disciples as a result of Holy Spirit's power.

c. How can you do greater works than Jesus did?

d. How did Peter keep others' adulation about him in perspective?

e. What does the story of the Good Samaritan teach?

9 a. What did Jesus say was the reason for this man's blindness?

b. Was the blind man sick because of sin?

c. What's the connection between sin and sickness, according to the Bible?

d. Give examples from the Old and New Testaments.

e. Where does obedience come from?

DISCUSSION: Which principle from stories of taking the roof off, healing the ten lepers, healing at Bethesda, or healing the blind man speaks most to you?

Chapter Three

Faith

ONE DAY IN SERVICE, THE LORD SHOWED ME A HEAD WITH TEN-drils, like fingers. That word exactly described a healing that was needed in someone's family. A lady in the congregation said her niece had recently been diagnosed with a brain tumor, which doctors had described like I did—as fingers spreading. We prayed intensely that morning, with faith in the Healer's ability to touch even a big thing like that. When the niece returned to the doctor, he pronounced the tumor gone. Another time, Wade and I were called to the hospital for a young man unable to communicate because of a drug overdose. We prayed in faith. He imme-diately came out of his comatose condition and carried on a conversation. Putting faith into action accomplishes even the impossible.

Faith. That word is polarizing, and teaching about it has produced much confusion and controversy. Some think faith is a cultish phenom-enon that gives people their selfish desires. Others, however, know if you have no faith, the teeth in your prayers are missing. Faith is crucial to receiving answered prayers; healings often elude you because you don't understand how it works. You pray formulas instead of faith or pray from a fear-based stance. God uses two types of faith for healing. The first is the gift of faith, which is part of Holy Spirit's gifts. As that faith is dropped into you, you have an unshakable confidence that God will heal. I'll talk about that type of faith more in Chapter Five. Jesus demonstrated the other kind of faith, which requires understanding the process to activate—believing, speaking, then acting (see 2 Cor. 4:13).

What Did Jesus Do?

Once, as Jesus and His disciples left Jericho, a great multitude followed. By the road, blind Bartimaeus sat begging (see Matt. 20:29-34; Mark 10:46-52; Luke 18:35-43). The gospels' details vary—Matthew says two blind men sat by the road, and Luke doesn't name the man. Bartimaeus heard a commotion. The crowd's volume prompted him to ask about the clamor (see Luke 18:36). When someone told Him Jesus was passing by, he grew excited and cried out, "Jesus, Son of David, have mercy on me!" (Mark 10:47). The throng cautioned him to be quiet, but he cried louder for Jesus' mercy. That second time, Jesus stopped and asked someone to call Bartimaeus to Him. Matthew says Jesus called the blind *men*, and Luke says He *commanded* the blind man be brought to Him (see Matt 20:32; Luke 18:40).

After Jesus called, Mark says people told Bartimaeus to "Be of good cheer. Rise, He is calling you" (Mark 10:49). As Bartimaeus heard, he hastened to obey—threw off his garment, rose, and rushed to Jesus (see Mark 10:50). Jesus asked, "What do you want Me to do for you?" (Mark 10:51). As he answered, the blind man called Him, "Rabboni" (Mark 10:51) and told Jesus he wanted to see. Matthew alone says Jesus had compassion and touched his/their eyes (see Matt. 20:34). In all versions, he/they received sight, but Mark adds that Jesus told Bartimaeus to go his way (see Mark 10:52). Mark and Luke say Jesus said he was healed because of his faith, and every version says sight was restored immediately, and the man/men followed Jesus down the road. Luke says as a result of the healing, the blind man glorified God, and other witnesses praised Him (see Luke 18:43).

Encouragement or Discouragement

Faith pervades Bartimaeus' story. Though the gospels had some different details, all versions showed a wonderful healing. The first principle I glean is that others can impact your miracle. I see two types of people in this event—discouragers and encouragers. When the Lord has fresh vision for you, satan plants discouragers to negate that. Discouragers were those who told Bartimaeus not to bother Jesus. If he'd listened, his miracle wouldn't have happened. Our pastor, Richard Ware, once said, "Attacks don't come about where you are but where you're going." Only you can ultimately determine where that is because when Jesus has something new for you, no one will understand it like you do. On the Road to Damascus, others experienced Paul's encounter, but no one's perception of what happened was exactly like his. One reference says others heard but didn't see. A later allusion relates the experience but says others saw but didn't hear (see Acts 9:7; 22:9). That tells me everyone will have an opinion about your experience with the Lord, but no one's perception will exactly parallel your own.

Getting vision for healing is crucial, but vision encompasses more than just physical healing. After Jesus healed another blind man, He spoke about religious people and lack of vision when He said He'd come to the world "that those who do not see may see, and that those who see may be made blind" (John 9:39). Bartimaeus demonstrated this concept. He was blind in his body, but his spirit had vision of what Jesus could do despite others' opinions. Your response to discouragers should mirror Bartimaeus'—cry out louder and harder because if you seek Him, you'll find Him (see Jer. 29:13). Crying out despite what discouragers say makes the difference between receiving or staying in your current circumstances.

Discouragers may fight your pursuit of fresh vision for any number of reasons—envy, fear your vision will exceed their own, lack of understanding. Some simply don't want you to succeed. They discouraged Bartimaeus similarly to today's religious folks who follow Jesus but don't want to hear something that will push them beyond their comfort zones. Many discouragers stifle others who seek expanded vision because they've always done things the same way. When Bartimaeus called out, discouragers who warned him to be quiet were "those who went before" (Luke 18:39). That wording is interesting. Sometimes those fighting the hardest to keep others from getting new sight are those who've been saved the longest and don't want things to change. They recognize the Lord but have never formed intimate relationship with the Healer. They pay lip service to Jesus' healing abilities and experience a healing "accident" now and then. However, because of inexperience, they don't know that calling out to Him won't disturb Him.

In contrast, encouragers want others to succeed in their quest for new vision. Encouragers don't operate with an agenda except to help. They're the ones who reassure others like when Bartimaeus' encouragers said, "Be of good cheer" as they brought him the Lord's message. After they shared Jesus' word with Bartimaeus, they helped him go to Jesus. They're the ones who guide others toward a closer experience with the Lord. They rejoice when good things happen to you, like some rejoiced about the healing of Bartimaeus. As encouragers guide you, they also give direction. Sometimes that may be through a hard word; but an encourager knows that for your vision to come to fruition, you must rise from your negative situations, your own beggar's garments, and ascend to a new level to get that vision. Encouragers can be the difference between success or failure in reaching the Lord and receiving what He has. Where do you fit? Are you a discourager or encourager?

Pressing In

When Bartimaeus heard Jesus was coming, he demonstrated faith by not wasting that opportunity to seek the Lord. Perseverance despite discouraging words or reactions can be the outcome's difference. Many desperate people whom Jesus healed pressed in despite others, likely rude and inconsiderate in their efforts to draw near the Healer for their own needs. You should emulate Bartimaeus and others who had valid reasons for not pressing in, but they still did and obtained a healing. Pressing in was difficult when his blindness limited mobility, bleeding made the woman unclean, and overcrowding created no access to Him except through the roof. Others likely criticized their persistence, but desperation made them press in despite circumstances and opinions. Though you seek quick fixes, pressing in isn't the easy route, and many want what's comfortable or requires the least effort. They don't keep trying if they're initially unsuccessful. Between prayer and healing coming to fruition, many get discouraged and give up rather than being assured that God's done a work that will be completed. Most accomplishments come as a result of pressing in through difficult circumstances—a college degree, medical breakthrough, life-changing invention, dire healing. Often, your answer comes as you ignore the hindrances, persistently draw nearer to Him, and press in for His touch.

Desperation brought the afflicted to Jesus' attention, but pressing in brought results. Bartimaeus and others had been sick a long time and had learned to accommodate their handicaps. You also may have become resigned to your situation and may not have attempted to change it, but then desperation drives you toward the Answer. Don't let go or stop pressing in until the Lord comes by, hears you, feels your desperation, and answers your pleas. Jesus responded to Bartimaeus' and others' faith and desperation with miracles. That tells me when it's hopeless, press in; He's there meeting needs of those who diligently call on Him. How much do you want to be healed? Can you follow Bartimaeus' example?

Many have forgotten how to press in—waiting on the Lord or falling on their faces to access that place where they can touch Him for theirs and others' needs. That secret place is your strength and protection when the enemy of sickness pursues. Worship takes you into that place and produces answers. Travail and Holy Spirit's gifts are also pressing-in tools to break through what's impeding healing. However, the key is determination to press in despite obstacles. Sometimes, that requires sacrifices—pushing back your plate, getting out of your cozy bed, not stopping before you reach the Master. You know He's the answer, so you press in beyond a quick-fix mindset because He's not in a hurry.

Jesus gave instructions for pressing in:

Ask, and it will be given to you; seek, and you will find; knock, and it will be opened to you. For everyone who asks receives, and he who seeks finds, and to him who knocks it will be opened (Matthew 7:7-8).

These words delineate the pressing-in process when a seeker doesn't give up but progressively pushes harder. Some stop after they ask; but for hard needs, you should also seek every avenue and knock on every door. That means you get in prayer lines, fast when you feel led, bury yourself in His Word, call intercessors, fall on your face, and keep your petitions before God. Jesus finished His instructions with promises: Askers will receive, seekers will find, and knockers will discover open doors. Perseverance makes your healing quest happen, just like with Bartimaeus.

Following the Process: Believing

The Bible speaks often about believing as a part of faith. Jesus referenced it as He healed the woman with the issue of blood, the centurion, the leper (see Matt. 9:22, 8:13; Luke 17:19). Once, blind men asked Jesus to heal them. He responded by inquiring if they believed that He could heal. After they said yes, He healed them because of their faith (see Matt. 9:27-31). When you know He's "able to do exceedingly abundantly above all that we ask or think" (Eph. 3:20), you can believe His ability will make that impossible healing happen. Bartimaeus showed his belief after he inquired about the crowd's noise. When he heard Jesus' name, he called out because he believed Jesus was the Healer. Sometimes you should check out what's making noise in the Kingdom and then fervently seek it. Believing is crucial; when combined with receiving, answers happen. He's the God of impossibilities (see Matt. 19:26).

The definitive faith scripture is self-explanatory: "Now faith is the substance of things hoped for, the evidence of things not seen" (Heb. 11:1). I like that this begins with the word *now*. Faith isn't something old but fresh and *now*. Faith has substance, *hupostasis,* meaning "a setting under (support)...essence...assurance...confidence."[1] Faith's essence is tangible and supports your pleas. With confidence, you can sink your teeth into the solid promise, hold it in your hand, and not let it go. Faith is when you're assured of something, so you visualize and believe in your spirit before you see it in the natural. Visualization is important. Remember when God told Abram to look and all he could see would be his (see Gen. 13:15)? Whatever you visualize, you can have through faith.

I like the definition that says *confidence*. Faith says you're healed despite how circumstances appear; in the meantime, you "do not cast away your confidence, which has great reward" (Heb. 10:35). Healing comes by confidence that the Lord will perform His promise. That faith substance says though you don't see it in the natural, you still believe the answer's there, like atoms, air, or gravity. Faith says even when facts tell you otherwise, healing is done. I like Paul's words discussing how people await God's redemption—with "earnest expectation" (Rom. 8:19). That describes Bartimaeus' anticipation of Jesus' capabilities and how you and I should await—expect it earnestly. Your physical eyes may not yet see results, but what you see with those eyes isn't God's reality and just temporary for those who walk in faith (see 2 Cor. 4:18).

When God told Abraham and Sarah they'd have a son, they received that word, had confidence in Him, and believed that their descendants would be numerous as sand (see Heb. 11:11-12). Before the promise's fulfillment, they didn't have daily communication and affirmation that Isaac was on his way. Many grow weary in that waiting phase (see Gal. 6:9) or if they haven't had confirmation in a while. Regardless of impossibilities, Abraham was "fully convinced that what He had promised He was also able to perform" (Rom. 4:21). He believed despite his promise taking twenty-five years to come to pass, but it eventually transpired because they stood on their promise. Though a hopeless situation, they refused to consider that Sarah was ninety and no longer capable of reproducing or that Abraham's 100-year-old body had its own limitations (see Rom. 4:19). They had faith in the Father. God loves impossible situations like Abraham's and Bartimaeus' because "things which are impossible with men are possible with God" (Luke 18:27). Through your impossibilities, He gets a chance to show His power, grace, and love.

Although Bartimaeus was healed instantly, your promise may take a while to come to pass. Abraham and other patriarchs, "died in faith, not having received the promises, but having seen them afar off were assured of them" (Heb. 11:13). I like that wording. Sometimes what you see in the Spirit is far off, but you can't give up. Although he lived to see his son born, Abraham and Sarah's promise was fulfilled through their grandson after their deaths. If Abraham had faltered instead of believing, the promise couldn't have been completed. He was so sure of

God's faithfulness that his faith "was accounted to him for righteousness" (Rom. 4:3). If his faith is an example of righteousness, then lack of faith must be unrighteousness. Faith is the basis for your answer; without it, pleasing God is impossible (see Heb. 11:6).

Believing plays a role in all aspects of your Christian walk. By faith, you know God created the worlds. By faith, you believe the Bible is alive and truly God's word. By faith you know Jesus is the Son of God who takes away your sins. By faith, you know God desires to heal His kids. Hebrews 11 describes how men and women of faith received their promises. Through faith they believed and received God's report even during the long time before evidence of the promise came (see Heb. 11:2). Biblical saints received their miracles because, "contrary to hope, in hope [they] believed" (Rom. 4:18). When you believe, you first receive in the heavenlies; then it becomes reality on earth because no matter what things look like, you don't walk by sight but rather by faith (see 2 Cor. 5:7). Therefore, before you have healing in the physical realm, you must receive certainty in your spirit. It's not the logical route, but it's the one that brings results.

Following the Process: Speaking

Your Words

Another aspect of receiving your answer is speaking words of faith. The psalmist paired these two concepts: "I believed, therefore I spoke" (Ps. 116:10). Believing is part of the equation, but speaking seals the believing because words are important. Once, Jesus declared, "If you have faith as a mustard seed, you can say to this mulberry tree, 'Be pulled up by the roots and be planted in the sea,' and it would obey you'" (Luke 17:6). Jesus followed the mustard seed analogy with a parable about servants (see Luke 17:7-10). Faith through your words is like a servant who, when hired to work, must follow your commands. As you speak, that servant, those words, must do what you've spoken. Therefore, though your throat feels sore, you speak and refuse sickness, and those words accomplish what you've proclaimed (see Isa. 55:11). Once we were headed to a family event in Texas when bad-looking clouds loomed ahead, the type that can produce tornadoes. I spoke to them that we wouldn't have any storms. The sky cleared, and I never thought about it during our rainfree drive until my brother called to check on us. Tornadoes had touched down after we passed through. Words matter.

If you have mountains like sickness to be removed, you must speak to them as part of the faith process. In His mustard-seed teaching, Jesus stressed "you can *say* to" the mountain to be removed. Mark's version refers to speaking three times (see Mark 11:23). Faith grows in your hearts as you believe then speak it. Solomon said you are what you think in your heart (see Prov. 23:7). Because from "the abundance of the heart [the] mouth speaks" (see Luke 6:45), if faith's in your heart, it comes from your mouth, and you *are* healed. Lack of faith in the heart comes out the mouth, too. Words about illnesses and recovery work hand in hand with attitude. Even tone and timing demonstrate your heart toward an impending healing. Your words to your children prophesy their future—they'll become doctors or teachers, instead of saying they're worthless. Similarly, words that speak faith or lack of faith frame your destiny.

Your body works on this principle. What you expect becomes a self-fulfilling prophecy—healing or sickness. If you believe then speak that you're getting a cold, you get one because you're justified or condemned by your words (see Matt. 12:37). Some people's words exalt illnesses louder than faith words that overcome the sickness, so you should speak healing, not the problem. You block or appropriate promises by your words; so bask in the positive and proclaim life, not death. Solomon said life and death are affected by the tongue (see Prov. 18:21), even others' words about you (see 1 Cor. 4:13). Because of that, you should be careful whom you tell about your sickness. Avoid those who'll drag you down to their weak-faith thinking. Instead, choose encouragers who understand, believe, and speak Christ's finished work.

Paul said since you have faith in Jesus, you "believe and therefore speak" (2 Cor. 4:13). Believing then speaking faith are both part of the healing equation. Like God "gives life to the dead and calls those things which do not exist as though they did" (Rom. 4:17), your words become reality through your confession. If you say you're sick, you are; if you say you're healed, by faith you are. That means by your confession you speak into situations, even by wording your declaration not to claim the sickness. Saying "my flu" instead of "the report of flu" gives you ownership. That's an important aspect of healing—being proactive instead of reactive. It's much easier to get victory over illnesses before they begin rather than after they've taken root in your body. If you assert your authority by refusing or not claiming sickness through your words, you walk in faith. By speaking that you refuse the enemy's ailment, your faith words derail his plans.

Crying Out

Bartimaeus' faith words mattered more than once. First, he cried out to Jesus. Healing happens when you cry out, tell Him your needs, and push in to touch Him or let Him touch you. David said, "O Lord my God, I cried out to You, and You healed me" (Ps. 30:2). Another time he needed God's help, and in his "distress [he] called upon the Lord, and cried out to [his] God; He heard [David's] voice" (Ps. 18:6). In a different psalm, Asaph also cried out to God, and He heard him (see Ps. 77:1). Crying out creates miracle dynamics, and saying His name changes everything. Without consideration of what others thought, Bartimaeus spoke his heart's words and adulation for the Lord as he cried out loudly for mercy. He screamed twice, so loudly he offended others' senses. People told him to be quiet, "but he cried out all the more" (Luke 18:39). Nothing Bartimaeus had done had brought an answer, but crying out to Jesus did. Sometimes your petitions may be loud and not pretty, but they work!

This Greek word for *cried* out is *krazo*, which means to "scream...call aloud (shriek, exclaim, intreat)."[2] I like *intreat*, or *entreat*. In that word is the element of begging the Lord. Bartimaeus entreated the Lord with a tool he already knew—begging. Now, a change of mindset had occurred because begging for his sustenance had become begging for his sight. Often when God brings fresh vision to your life, He uses your past experiences. However, in the past, those beggarly elements made you a victim. In Him, your experiences will work for Kingdom advancement as you become a victor. That includes entreating Him doggedly for your healing. Many pray but rarely cry out to beg the Master for His touch. You often settle for too little; then Jesus comes by, and everything changes. Tirelessly crying out catches His attention, so if the collective church as well as individuals scream for Him, expect transformation.

Jesus stopped after He heard the shrieks (see Mark 10:49). Think of that. Your cries make Him stand still and listen to your pleas. After He stopped, He sent for Bartimaeus, who didn't hesitate but hurried to respond to His calling. When Jesus summons, your attitude should change as you throw off your victim mentality—blindness, preconceived notions, poverty, or anything else inhibiting you from running to Him. You can't stay in that position if you want change. However, along with your cries, you must tell Jesus your need. When Bartimaeus "had come near, He asked him, saying 'What do you want Me to do for you?'" (Luke 18:40-41). Jesus spoke directly to Bartimaeus and told him to say what he wanted.

Bartimaeus had drawn near to Jesus. Though coming near positions you for healing, you still need to ask. From his own mouth, Bartimaeus had cried aloud for mercy, but he also needed to speak his healing need. As Jesus passes, tell Him what He can do for you. You don't get answers if you don't ask (see James 4:2). Obviously, Jesus knew his need, but Bartimaeus had to say it from his own mouth and not through intercessors. Others are a wonderful and necessary part of your Christian walk. We're told to bear one another's burdens (see Gal. 6:2). At times you should approach the church elders for prayer (see James 5:14). Intercessors carried Jesus' message to Bartimaeus and led him to Jesus after He called. However, many rely on others to talk to Jesus for them. Eventually, you can't rely on your pastor, mother, or grandma to call out to or approach Jesus for you. You must ask for yourself. Bartimaeus' words of faith made healing happen when he spoke his specific need: "Lord, that I may receive my sight" (Luke 18:41). After this, Jesus responded by touching and healing his eyes. Calling out and speaking your requests has power to manifest healing. Bartimaeus received exactly what he asked for when he screamed—mercy—and now he got a healing.

Following the Process: Acting

You put legs on your faith when you act because you don't just hear but also do the word [*logos*] (see James 1:22). Jesus sent people to tell Bartimaeus to come to Him, and they reported that Jesus told him to "Rise" (Mark 10:49). If He calls you, the appropriate response is to rise and go because faith requires obedience in addition to believing, speaking, and acting. "Rise" is *egeiro,* with several meanings, including to "rouse (lit. from sleep, from sitting or lying, from disease, from death)."[3] Bartimaeus had literally been sitting or lying in his begging stance. In the throes of despair, he probably felt contemptible or irrelevant to those who passed him each day. Does that describe how you sometimes feel— you don't matter to anyone? The longer you remain in that state, you become accustomed it, so your nature thinks that's your fate. Staying too long in adverse physical, spiritual, and emotional circumstances results in spiritual or physical death, while Jesus brings life. Bartimaeus had to rise to be freed from begging and disease. Rising changes your perspective so you can see from Jesus' point of view. If you want change, you can't keep sitting in your circumstances.

After Bartimaeus rose and went to Jesus, the Lord healed him and told him to go his way (see Mark 10:52)—stop begging, be healed, start a new life. Hannah also had to make that choice to act on the man of God's word. She was in desperate straits in the temple, sobbing and not eating. Then, she clutched on to Eli's promise and let faith kick in. She spoke faith words, left, ate, changed her sad expression, rose in the morning, worshiped, and went home (see 1 Sam. 1:7, 18-19). If Hannah had stayed in her grieving stance and not gone home to her husband, she couldn't have become impregnated with God's purpose. When Jesus met the ten lepers in Samaria and Galilee (see Luke 17:12-19), like Bartimaeus, they called for Jesus to have mercy on them. He told them to go to the priests and show themselves; and "as they went, they were cleansed" (Luke 17:14). Acting on His word made them clean as they obeyed. Your faith must be active: "as the body without the spirit is dead, so faith without works is dead" (James 2:26). If God tells you to do something, your job is to obey.

The Hebrews 11 saints acted upon God's word before their promises' completion. Abel offered, Noah prepared, Abraham obeyed and went (see Heb. 11:4, 7, 8). In Jesus' miracles, the man with a withered hand stretched it out; the man at Bethesda rose, took up his bed, and walked (see Matt. 12:13; John 5:8). Bartimaeus rose, threw off his rags, and went to Jesus. With disciples, people brought the sick into the streets so Peter's shadow might fall on them and heal them. Peter stepped from the boat (see Acts 5:15; Matt. 14:29). The crippled man at Lystra leaped up and walked as Paul instructed (see Acts 14:8-10). People brought handkerchiefs and aprons that had touched Paul's body, and they were healed and delivered (see Acts 19:11-12). Each example demonstrates that faith requires action for a miracle to occur. Whatever God tells you to do, acting is crucial. Faith requires all—believing, speaking, and acting.

Larry, my brother-in-law, grew up poor with nine of his thirteen siblings still living in their single-parent household. His mother was a woman of faith who devoured God's Word, trusted in His ability, and knew that seeing answers to her faith required action. She had a saying: "Make preparation to receive your blessing." When her family needed meat, she'd send the kids out to glean corn or horse weeds in already-harvested fields for their yet-to-come pig or cow. The Lord never disappointed and provided so much fodder that the farmer of the field was amazed at how much the children found. Then someone always showed up with a delicious answer to prayer. Her mantra applied to healing, also. Her young daughter had polio and couldn't attend school for two years. That year, before school started, his mother and her prayer group interceded for the little girl and knew God had answered. The next day his mom prepared to receive the blessing. She made a pattern, bought fabric, and sewed school dresses for her little girls, even her baby who was still gnarled and unable to walk. A couple nights later, that lame child gingerly walked to her mother's bedside and complained that her legs were hurting. Putting faith into action by preparing to receive saw her daughter start school that fall—healed!

Growing Your Faith

Although God's given each a faith portion, ever since Jesus' time, some have wanted more. Jesus gave the mustard seed example in response to apostles asking Him to increase their faith (see Luke 17:6). He had previously used the analogy of the mustard seed to teach about the Kingdom of heaven. After they were unable to cast out demons, He said if you have faith proportionate to the mustard seed, "nothing will be impossible for you" (Matt. 17:20). Nothing! Not delivering from demons, not eradicating poverty, not healing sickness. Although He implied that great accomplishments happen with a small amount of faith, the seed itself teaches much. Within that seed is potential to become that great tree.

Though it's the least of seeds, once it's planted, it grows large (see Luke 13:18-19). Beginning exceptionally smaller than most seeds, its success is in the planting and nurturing. It grows rapidly but takes a while to mature and bear fruit. Then, despite its small beginnings, its branches spread wide and become large enough to climb in and for birds to nest in.[4] Like the mustard seed, your seed of faith must be well-planted, then nurtured and allowed time to germinate. Then it should grow fast and ultimately bear fruit. Have you become a solid Christian whose roots are deep and arms are raised in prayer and as a support for others? I like the saying, "No root, no fruit." The deeper your roots grow in Him, the more fruit you have to give others. You get answers as you plant your feet firmly and stand in faith, determination, and stubbornness. During the growth period, faith must be watered with Holy Spirit and the Word and weeds of doubt pulled up.

Faith grows in many ways—voraciously reading the Word, focusing regularly on prayer time, experiencing Holy Spirit for yourself, tenaciously holding on to your promises. Because faith works through love (see Gal. 5:6), more love equals more faith. It also grows by sharing testimonies of God's past works (see Luke 8:39). However, an important, but not-too-popular way faith grows is through adversity. Hardships can be a stumbling block or a huge growth tool as you're refined and tested in "the furnace of affliction" (Isa. 48:10). I love that picture of the Lord heating things up so He can change and purify you to create growth. We dislike the idea, but trials are crucial to crafting qualities like perseverance, character, and hope (see Rom. 5:3-4). I like that perseverance is mentioned here. The more you persevere, the more you know He's your strength and better understand His faithfulness. Therefore, run to adversity, not away from it.

Many Christians are excited about God's promises in their salvation package. However, along with your promise comes a problem—those parable-of-the-sower birds that try to steal the word you received (see Mark 4:4). If your faith isn't planted properly, it's susceptible to adverse circumstances—hungry birds, hot sun, winds that blow it away. If your seeds are well-planted, life's storms will make them grow. Remember when Joseph got a promise through a dream about his brothers and father bowing to him? Before that could happen, he was looking up at them from a pit and endured much before he arrived at his destiny (see Gen. 37:24). My husband often quotes Smith Wigglesworth that great faith grows through great fights. Trials are part of your Christian landscape. Faith increases as you trust and give trials to Him.

Bartimaeus' adversities had been blindness, begging, discouragement from others, and everything that accompanies those. Because he had no ability on his own, he knew Jesus was his only answer. He'd obviously heard of and believed in the Lord because he responded as soon as he heard Jesus' name. That seed of belief in Jesus had taken root. However, hearing about Him and encountering Him personally are different. Those who know God only on a cognitive level and not through experience lack great insight into what He can do. Bartimaeus' life changed when he actually met Jesus. Experiencing His mighty capabilities produces great faith and expectation that miracles will occur. As a result, faith takes a deeper root. By the way, "iron sharpens iron" (Prov. 27:17). If you want more faith, hang out with those who have great faith.

His Faithfulness

Faith grows each time you trust in His faithfulness. Many tell us about their problems, from infertility to marital issues to financial woes to healing needs. My advice is always the same—trust Him. When you don't know what to do, trust Him. For insurmountable problems, trust Him. Faith grows by trusting because you learn more about His faithfulness. After you realize that "The Lord is not slack concerning His promise" (2 Pet. 3:9), you can stand fast despite what your eye perceives. He's always faithful, a difficult concept for humans to understand. Do you know anyone who unfailingly puts your interests first? Probably not, but God does just that. He's faithful and able to fix whatever comes along—doctors' pronouncements, judges' verdicts, bosses' unfairness, or nature itself. Nothing supersedes God's faithfulness.

Jesus performed many signs, wonders, and miracles because He had confidence that whatever He asked, God would give. With that same certainty in the Father, great miracles are still available. Because the Shunammite woman knew He was faithful after fulfilling His promise of a son (see 2 Kings 4), she didn't give up when her child died. By a miracle, she'd conceived, so she knew God wouldn't give her a baby and then take him back. Her faith saw her boy raised from the dead. If He gives you a promise, God's answer to your prayer is "Yes and...Amen" (see 2 Cor. 1:20), and He won't renege and take that promise back.

After the children arrived in the Promised Land, God told Joshua to have each tribe lay down a stone as a remembrance for future generations of Jordan's waters being cut off and God delivering them (see Josh. 4:7). Jesus alluded to memorial pillars when He questioned disciples who forgot to take bread with them in the boat. He asked if they didn't remember or understand the lesson of feeding the multitudes (see Mark 8:13-21). God gives memorial pillars for you to remember your own examples of His faithfulness. Healings, miracles, and life's occurrences remind you of God's ability to answer the next time. When my sister's problems overwhelmed her, she called our mother for prayer. Mom assured her, "It hasta happen. I remember the spot on the wall where I was lookin' when God gave me that promise." I have many of my own spots on the wall, my memorial pillars, to recall wilderness experiences, God's faithfulness, and His ability to keep what I've given Him, yet again (see 2 Tim. 1:12).

Once, I'd been having terrible finger pain. Wade felt led to have a healing service at our Times of Refreshing meeting. As a woman of God prayed for me, I was slain in the Spirit and lay travailing. For a few weeks after that, my fingers kept hurting, but I used my mother's words. I recalled the spot on the floor where I was slain as He healed me. I knew

God was doing a work, even though it wasn't complete. My fingers eventually got well and stayed well. Confidence and faith grow by reflecting on what He's done. If you're convinced "the Lord is faithful, who will establish you and guard you from the evil one" (2 Thess. 3:3), the evil of sickness is healed by that faithfulness. You can be sure that "He who promised is faithful" (Heb. 10:23).

Conclusion

Once, a TV interviewer asked for examples of healings we'd experienced. I answered that so many had happened that my relating just one was difficult. However, a recent miracle occurred because of faith. I wasn't working on the altar team one Wednesday night, but Jean came down to my seat for prayer during ministry time. She'd acted on the Lord's leading to come to me for a burning in her hip; the doctor was treating her for what could potentially be wrong, one possibility being shingles. I had faith for that because I knew God loves to heal that ailment. I'd been healed of shingles more than twenty years earlier. As I prayed in faith, I spoke for whatever it could be, including shingles, to be eradicated. The next day, she called me, excitedly. Those blisters had begun to dry up that night. The next day, the doctor confirmed the diagnosis; before she could take the medicine, the shingles had dried up and were gone.

Faith. What a simple yet profound word! With each trial that challenges your belief system, faith grows so you'll be ready for your next challenge. If you understand that His faithfulness is in response to your faith, you don't have one defining healing but multiple, regular healings for and through you. He's just waiting to heal you, but you must press in despite what others say or think. Then, cry out to Him. Circumstances, symptoms, and emotions may say otherwise, but you should "know that the Lord your God, He *is* God, the faithful God who keeps covenant and mercy for a thousand generations with those who love Him and keep His commandments" (Deut. 7:9). When believing, speaking, and acting are part of your character, healing's a reality in your Christian walk.

Questions to Ponder

Answers in the Appendix

1   a.   Explain the terms *encouragers* and *discouragers*.

      b.   Give the types of vision people may seek.

      c.   Why do discouragers want to keep others from getting fresh vision?

      d.   How did Bartimaeus' encouragers uplift him?

      e.   Have you experienced these groups? Explain. Which category do you fall into?

2   a.   What obstacles did others overcome to press in?

      b.   Fill in the blanks: ___ brought the ___ to ___ ___, but ___ ___ brought ___.

      c.   Give examples of how you could also press in to Jesus for your answer.

      d.   What are the pressing-in steps Jesus lists in Matthew 7:7-8?

3   a.   Explain Hebrews 11:1 and how the definitions for *substance* fit with that scripture.

      b.   What were adversities Abraham and Sarah faced which could've impacted their answer if they'd dwelt on them?

      c.   Abraham's faith was so strong, that it was considered what?

      d.   How does your Christian walk demonstrate faith on many levels?

4   a.   How are words like a servant?

      b.   How do words fit with mustard seed faith?

      c.   How can speaking facilitate or hinder your healing?

      d.   What does the author mean by saying to be proactive instead of reactive about your healing?

5   a.   Besides words that indicate how loudly you cry out, what does the word for crying out also mean?

       b.   How does that meaning show a change of mindset for Bartimaeus?

       c.   How did Jesus respond to Bartimaeus' cries?

       d.   What did Jesus ask Bartimaeus to tell Him?

       e.   Why must you speak your need?

6   a.   What message did intercessors bring Bartimaeus from Jesus?

       b.   Why was his compliance with this message important?

       c.   How did Hannah also act on the word of the Lord?

       d.   Give other biblical examples of those who received their promise after they acted.

7   a.   Jesus' analogy of the mustard seed is mentioned more than once in this chapter. How does that seed teach about growing your faith?

       b.   What does the author say are ways to grow in faith? Do you have an example of when adversities made you grow?

       c.   What does the author mean when she says, "Those who know God only on a cognitive level and not through experience lack great insight into what He can do"?

8   a.   From this book or your own reading, give two biblical examples of God's faithfulness.

       b.   What are memorial pillars, and when did God have His people set them up?

       c.   What did those pillars represent? Give examples of how God's been faithful to you.

DISCUSSION: The story of Bartimaeus is familiar to most people. Give something about this chapter that spoke to you.

Chapter Four

Authority

One night I was awakened from a dream with the Lord saying, "Stomp on MRSA." I put that word on Facebook and had several responses from amazed people who were unsuccessfully battling that ailment. At our service a couple nights later, we acted on that word of knowledge and exercised our authority. We got an attitude against the enemy and stomped, as a prophetic action, in the front of the church—on MRSA and other things Holy Spirit brought to our minds. One lady reported that after a surgery, her incision had developed MRSA and wasn't responding to treatment. She needed another surgery. After the Lord spoke to stomp on MRSA, when she went for surgery, doctors found *no* infection. Another man's wife saw that message and was amazed because he'd developed MRSA and treatments weren't helping. Later she told me when he'd gotten better. It was after our stomping session.

Authority is a subject most understand and respect. If you go to school, a court procedure, or an airplane trip, you're surrounded by authority figures. Whether a policeman, pastor, parent, signaler on road construction, or manager in the grocery, you know to whom you must defer. Authority demands respect and action in your daily life, and ignoring that authority comes with consequences. Authority is an important spiritual concept, too. Because authority is part of your daily life, you can apply that understanding to your spiritual authority. Jesus had authority; and through Him you do, too.

What Did Jesus Do?

Jesus arrived at Capernaum, and a centurion told him his servant lay paralyzed and tormented at his house. He wanted Jesus to heal that servant (see Matt. 8:5-13; Luke 7:1-10). In Luke, he sent Jewish elders to Jesus, who pled for Him to heal the centurion's beloved servant who was near death. Jesus said He'd come to his home and heal the servant, but the centurion balked and declared himself unworthy for Jesus to come. Other Jews, however, told Jesus the centurion *was* deserving—he loved their nation and had built a synagogue. Jesus went toward the centurion's home (in Luke). In Matthew, Jesus and the centurion had a one-on-one conversation; Luke says as He neared the home, the centurion sent friends a second time to tell Jesus not to come because of his unworthiness. He added that he hadn't come to Jesus himself because he felt undeserving. He said if Jesus spoke the word, his servant would be healed.

When the centurion saw the Lord, he stated something that touched Jesus. This man explained that he understood how authority operated. As a leader of soldiers, he was a man of authority himself, commanding soldiers who obeyed his orders. Whether directing soldiers or servants, when he gave orders for them to go, to come, or to do, they were obliged to obey. Having had that experience, he knew Jesus had the same authority, but spiritual rather than military; when He spoke, sickness had to obey. These words amazed and pleased Jesus. He marveled and told the crowd He had "not found such great faith, not even in Israel" (Matt.

8:10). Then, Matthew records that He followed with a prophetic word that sometime Gentiles would come in while many Jews would be left behind. After that, Jesus told this Gentile centurion to "Go [his] way; and as [he had] believed, so let it be done" (Matt. 8:13). As they returned to the house, they heard the servant had been healed when Jesus spoke those words.

Humility Like Jesus

The centurion's story has much to teach about Jesus' authority for healing. Humility is a facet of love as you prefer and seek to help others, even those with lower earthly status. The centurion loved others enough to pursue Jesus desperately, even for his servant. That should speak to you because he perceived the servant's healing was his responsibility. Jesus understood both humility and deep love for others because He personified both. Jesus Himself loved and was humble, and none of His recorded healings were for those who thought their position or person entitled them to greater access to Him. The centurion's humility made him feel unworthy for Jesus to come to his house. However, despite feeling undeserving, he still approached Jesus. I've heard many comment about their unworthiness like this centurion, but some let that feeling keep them from seeking Jesus. How often do you miss Jesus' blessing because you think He wouldn't heal someone like you? He's ready and willing to come to where you are and meet your needs.

Unlike his self-perception, others described the centurion as "deserving" (Luke 7:4). People are watching, and these Jews recognized he obviously loved God and His people. Too many tout their own accomplishments instead of remembering to "Let another man praise you, and not your own mouth" (Prov. 27:2). Luke says if you're invited to a feast, "sit down in the lowest place" (Luke 14:10). If you promote yourself, God doesn't have an opportunity to elevate you. Peter says, if you're humble, God can exalt you in His time (see 1 Pet. 5:6). Although he wasn't a Jew, the centurion had demonstrated his love for God. God hears, heals, and delivers those who love Him. The psalmist wrote God's words that apply to this centurion: "Because he has set his love upon Me, therefore I will deliver him; I will set him on high, because he has known My name" (Ps. 91:14).

The centurion reminds me of Cornelius. Though he also was a centurion in the Roman army, he loved God, regularly prayed, and gave alms to the poor (see Acts 10:2). One day God sent an angel who called Cornelius' name and told him his prayers had been heard, and his alms had come before the Lord. Words are fine, but demonstrating those words speaks volumes to others and to God and opens heaven's doors for blessings. The word *alms* is *eleemosune*, which means "compassionateness, i.e. (as exercised to the poor)."[1] Your helping those in need doesn't go unnoticed because God loves giving. He expects you to tithe, but beyond that is what you give cheerfully because of a compassionate heart toward the church, ministries, and others. God keeps a record because giving alms shows your heart. He promises to supply your *needs*, but you can have much more by sowing seeds of love (see 2 Cor. 9:6).

When the Lord says He'll give to you as a result of your giving, healing is one thing you reap. I once heard, "You can give without loving, but you can't love without giving." How appropriate that loving and giving go together because the Father demonstrated that concept. God *loved* the world so much that He *gave* His Son. Giving is a reflection of God's love for you and your love for Him and others. When it comes to receiving rewards like healing, your actions reach the Lord's ear. Do you know His name, and does He know yours? Like both centurions, do people and the Lord know your heart by your deeds?

His Authority

After the centurion said he understood authority based on his military experience, Jesus described the centurion as demonstrating the greatest faith He'd witnessed. He'd seen others' faith often, so this comment speaks to me. Understanding authority is key to faith and healing. Authority is having a legal right to do something. In the Garden, God gave man dominion in the earth (see Gen. 1:26), so "The heaven[s]... are the Lord's; but the earth He has given to the children of men" (Ps. 115:16). God put everything under man's feet, in subjection to him (see Heb. 2:8) and made all creatures on earth tamed by humans (see James 3:7). God gave man authority here on earth, and He doesn't take a gift back. Because of man's dominion, God needed to deal with earth through a man. Therefore, His Son was sent to conquer death, but Jesus couldn't do that in His deity. He became human to operate here with legal authority in a flesh body.

Because of His legal authority, Jesus could speak His words into existence and demonstrated this with every need that arose—sickness, demons, death, even nature bowed to Him. David said, "You rule the raging of the sea; when its waves rise, You still them" (Ps. 89:9). This phenomenon occurred as He travelled with His disciples in a boat (see Matt. 8:24-26). A violent storm with massive, menacing waves covered the boat and frightened disciples. Jesus didn't fret, though, because He was "asleep on a pillow" (Mark 4:38) and slept soundly during the ordeal. Does that speak to you? If your life's storms don't disturb Jesus' peaceful slumber on His pillow, why should they worry you? When they do, you should emulate disciples who knew the storm would be stilled when they called on the Master. When Jesus rebuked the storm, disciples marveled how even nature would "obey Him" (see Matt. 8:26-27). The Greek word used for *obey* was *hupakouo,* "To hear as a subordinate."[2] Doesn't the use of the word *subordinate* remind you of the centurion's comment about authority? Storms of life are subordinate to you like the centurion's soldiers and servants and therefore must be subject and respond to you as Jesus' representative. Waves of sickness and disease must obey their Creator's authority.

The psalmist talked of that authority: "For He spoke, and it was done; He commanded, and it stood fast" (Ps. 33:9). His authority created no other response but compliance to His word. Jesus asserted authority often, such as when He left the temple and saw a woman with a spirit of infirmity. She was bent over and unable to rise for eighteen years. He proclaimed, "Woman, you are loosed from your infirmity" (Luke 13:12). He laid hands on her, and she immediately stood up straight (see Luke 13:10-13). Another time He'd taught in the temple, and a man with unclean spirits crying out loudly caught His attention. Jesus rebuked the spirits, told them to be quiet, and ordered them to come out. They convulsed the man but came out without hurting him. Bystanders were amazed at His authority and power (see Luke 4:33-36). Jesus' authority was for everything—from nature to sickness to demons to death. How can anything be withheld when all things are yours through His authority?

Believers' Authority

New Testament uses of power are usually one of two kinds—authority and power. Holy Spirit's power is *dunamis,* which I'll discuss in Chapter Five. *Exousia* is believers' authority because of Jesus. It's often translated as *power* and defined by words like *force.* When Jesus appointed His twelve to walk with Him, preach, and have power (*exousia*) to heal sicknesses and cast out demons (see Mark 3:14-15), He was talking about another meaning for *exousia:* "delegated influence—authority, jurisdiction."[3] He explained this: "Do you not believe that I am in the Father, and the Father in Me? The words that I speak to you I do not speak on My own authority; but the Father who dwells in Me does the works" (John 14:10). Like Jesus had all authority because the Father was in Him, He delegated *exousia* to disciples and others when He called the seventy and gave them power because so many needed to be healed (see Luke 10:1). He assigned "power [*exousia*] over unclean spirits, to cast them out, and to heal all kinds of sickness and all kinds of disease" (Matt.

10:1). Now you have Holy Spirit's power and Jesus' authority over nature, demons, diseases, death (see Matt. 10:8). You're His representative and have a right to confront situations, apply that authority, and see results.

Jesus gave "authority to trample on serpents and scorpions, and over the power of the enemy, and nothing shall by any means hurt you" (Luke 10:19). Though believers' authority here is *exousia*, the enemy's power here is *dunamis*, strong power to wreak havoc. However, this scripture puts his power and your authority into perspective. If all you had were Jesus' authority (*exousia*), it defeats satan's *dunamis* every time as you assert authority in Him. By yourself, you have no power; with Jesus standing behind you, your words carry the weight of His authority. Your role in Jesus demands that the enemy of sickness must obey. *Exousia* gives victory for healing; then add Holy Spirit's *dunamis* to it—unbeatable! When you claim and use His Son's authority, the Lord makes your enemy "flee before you seven ways" (Deut. 28:7). Wow!

His Word

Our authority comes three ways—His word, His name, and His blood. First, if you want faith to grow or if you need healing, getting a word from God is crucial because "faith comes by hearing, and hearing by the word of God" (Rom. 10:17). That use of *word* in this scripture is *rhema*. You may have read a *logos* scripture many times; but because the Word (*logos*) is alive (see Heb. 4:12), one day that same scripture strikes your heart. Then, the *logos* settles into your spirit as a *rhema*. Your personal *rhema* may also come from other sources, including dreams, prophetic words, visions, a knowing in your spirit, a life event, or something you hear or read. When that happens, that *rhema* is His direct word for that moment or situation. As you contemplate that word, His promise becomes real, and the *rhema* creates breakthrough. It's a *now* word! As you trust God to do what His word says, your faith grows by holding fast to the promise. Jesus is the Word who paid the price.

Although the enemy entices you to waver, faith in His *rhema* helps you hold on to your healing.

Both the *rhema* and *logos* are powerful. Jeremiah compares God's word to strong tools when He says, "'Is not My word like a fire?' says the Lord, 'And like a hammer that breaks the rock in pieces'" (Jer. 23:29). You can use His word to burn away or break up hard things because He's faithful to perform His "good word toward you" (Jer. 29:10). His *good word* may be healing, your family's salvation, marital wholeness, financial prosperity. Peter says "the word [*rhema*] of the Lord endures forever" (1 Pet. 1:25). Your *rhema* is forever, so count on it. Despite your problem's severity, miracle needed, or events that could cause doubt, rest upon His promises and judge Him faithful to His word when He says, "I will perform that good thing which I have promised" (Jer. 33:14).

The enemy understands the power of God's word, so he tries to trick you with a perverted version of the Word. The serpent twisted the Word to Eve (see Gen. 3:4-5); in the wilderness during Jesus' trials, satan also distorted God's Word. Everyone should apply His word with integrity and not allow the enemy to misrepresent it to ensnare you or twist it yourself to suit personal agendas. When tempted, Jesus warred with God's true Word, proclaiming, "It is written," three times (see Matt. 4:1-11). After that, the devil left, and angels ministered to Him. The enemy still manipulates God's word to keep you from getting healed. However, when you receive your *rhema,* know your rights, and hold on to the word, no matter what the enemy does you're victorious. A few years back, I had psoriasis badly on my legs and arms. Then my friend Amanda gave me a scripture that became my *rhema:* "Every plant which My heavenly Father has not planted will be uprooted" (Matt. 15:13). Every time I'd see a mark, I'd quote my *rhema;* after a while, those marks were permanently gone. God's Word is a powerful weapon when you speak and believe it then let the Word do the work.

When you find a scripture that becomes a *rhema* for your need, you can appropriate it: memory (see Prov. 10:7), finances (see Ps. 112:3), weak bones (see Prov. 3:7-8), worry (see 1 Pet. 5:7), rest (see Ps. 116:7), strength (see Phil. 4:13), and so many others you can claim for victory. Standing on His *rhema* is fertile ground where your prayers can take root. I love Jesus' parable of the sower who planted seed in several situations (see Matt. 13:3-8; Mark 4:3-8; Luke 8:5-8). Some was sown where nothing allowed it to grow, so birds ate it immediately. Other seed fell on stony ground with little earth; so though it sprang up, it had no substance and was burned up by the sun. Some fell among thorns that choked it out, but others fell on good ground and thus yielded a wonderful crop. The word [*logos*] is that seed, which becomes your promise, and how it's received varies (see Mark 4:14).

Through the parable Luke describes different types of receivers (see Luke 8:1-15). Some believe enough to come forward for prayer but still don't get healed because they allow satan to steal that healing. As they leave, their words or expressions indicate doubt or non-acceptance. As a result, their healing probably won't happen. Others believe at first; but their faith is weak, so delay of the healing harvest discourages them, and they relinquish their miracle. Their soil was infertile for healing, so it's stolen when circumstances heat up—pain is still bad or the doctor's report is worse. As tribulation arises, they stumble (see Matt. 13:21) in their faith walk. The third group is those who allow the world's cares or other people to block the word from becoming their *rhema*. Finally, those who receive healings are the last group for whom God's word finds fertile ground. They understand that "unless a grain of wheat falls into the ground and dies, it remains alone; but if it dies, it produces much grain" (John 12:24). Healing may be delayed as it takes root in productive ground; during that time, they don't negate their promise.

Bartimaeus is part of this last group because he knew how to receive. Jesus told Bartimaeus: "Receive your sight; your faith has made you well"

(Luke 18:42). This statement shows what brought his healing to fruition. Jesus spoke to Bartimaeus, and he received the Lord's word. He didn't accept negative reports or hindrances from those around him. Instead, when Jesus told him to be healed, he believed. Knowing God's promises and standing on them makes you free (see John 8:31-32). The flip side is not knowing your promises; if you don't know, you can be destroyed (see Hos. 4:6). Many water down God's Word to meet their experiences instead of raising their expectations to meet His Word. Don't settle for less than He's given! If you know and believe the power associated with His "exceedingly great and precious promises" (2 Pet. 1:4), you can confidently war against the enemy with Jesus' words in the wilderness: "It is written." Being prepared with His Word, you can battle by suiting up each day in God's armor then standing on His promises (see Eph. 6:13). With His defensive warfare gear on, you can endure regardless of what appears to be true. Then you take the offensive weapon in your arsenal—"the sword of the Spirit, the word [*rhema*] of God" (Eph. 6:17). A *rhema,* sharper than any earthly sword, pierces any situation.

You receive *rhema* and hold on to it confidently as you say healing scriptures:

> *For I will restore health to you and heal you of your wounds* (Jeremiah 30:17).

> *My son, give attention to my words...keep them in the midst of your heart; for they are life to those who find them, and health to all their flesh* (Proverbs 4:20-22).

> *If you abide in Me, and My words abide in you, you will ask what you desire, and it shall be done for you* (John 15:7).

> *No weapon formed against you shall prosper* (Isaiah 54:17).

Believe and don't waver about His promises, because "Heaven and earth will pass away, but [His] words [*logos*] will by no means pass away" (Luke 21:33).

The Name of Jesus

The second way you have authority is through the name of Jesus. Because of His name and Holy Spirit, you were justified (see 1 Cor. 6:11), so you can approach the Father. While on earth, Jesus gave a formula for getting answered prayers: "Most assuredly, I say to you, whatever you ask the Father in My name He will give you. Until now you have asked nothing in My name. Ask, and you will receive" (John 16:23-24). Like David approached Goliath in the name of the Lord of Hosts (see 1 Sam. 17:45), when you draw near God through the name of His Son, power accompanies you. After His resurrection, Jesus told disciples about the power and authority in His name (see Mark 16:17-18). When He taught about greater works, He specified to ask in His name (see John 14:12-14). After Bartimaeus called upon Jesus' name (see Mark 10:47), things happened.

The book of Acts demonstrates how to use Jesus' name as your authority. First century church members suffered persecution for preaching and speaking His name but weren't deterred in their assignments. As a result, they saw mighty miracles. Peter and John's stories intrigue me because they had more than a passing acquaintance with Him. They'd loved Him, traveled with Him, and forged a close relationship as part of His inner circle. They'd witnessed firsthand His authority and knew His name gave power to accomplish great miracles. After the lame man's healing at the Gate Beautiful (see Acts 3:7), they clarified that the healing had nothing to do with their power but rather Jesus' name, because their "faith in His name, ha[d] made this man strong...Yes, the faith which *comes* through Him has given him this perfect soundness" (Acts 3:16). It's His name.

They picked up the mantle to preach Jesus to men for salvation and healing at great risk to themselves. They were arrested after healing that lame man then preaching Jesus and seeing 5,000 saved (see Acts 3:7; 4:4). As a result, a great assembly of religious leaders grilled them and asked, "By what power or by what name have you done this?" (Acts 4:7). That word *name* is *onoma*, "[authority, character]—called."[4] These religious folks knew if they preached or healed, it had to be in someone's authority. The unconverted Saul persecuted Christians in the priests' authority (see Acts 9:2). Those religious leaders came in the name and authority of Caiaphas or Caesar or Herod or Pilate. Names held authority. After that question, Peter responded "that by the name of Jesus Christ of Nazareth, whom you crucified, whom God raised from the dead, by Him this man stands here before you whole" (Acts 4:10). In Hebrew culture, a name couldn't be separated from the person it represented. Therefore, disciples calling upon Jesus Christ was the very anointing of Jesus' person, which came by His name.[5] His ability was their ability and authority to tap into. His name is "far above...every name that is named" (Eph. 1:21). What authority is in that name!

That Gate Beautiful healing brought other opportunities to declare His name's power and authority. As they were released following the healing, Peter and John were told not to speak or teach in Jesus' name (see Acts 4:18). This is so like the enemy to attempt to keep powerful tools from accomplishing healings in hearts and bodies. Peter and John knew their Power Source was responsible for all miracles and said, "We cannot but speak the things which we have seen and heard" (Acts 4:20). They'd experienced the great power and authority inherent in Jesus' name. Though they were physically threatened, they didn't back down and later prayed for *more* courage to continue preaching and healing in His name:

> *Lord...grant to Your servants that with all boldness they*
> *may speak Your word, by stretching out Your hand to heal,*

and that signs and wonders may be done through the name
of Your holy Servant Jesus (Acts 4:29-30).

Despite consequences, they wanted to be emboldened to speak His name to perform even more signs and wonders. Men who took up Jesus' calling could do so with confidence because of whom they'd trusted.

Jesus told disciples they were chosen and appointed to bear fruit that would remain; and that whatever they asked the Father in His name, He'd give it (see John 15:16). Because of your right to apply Jesus' name, you also can bear fruit as you take charge over satan. Jesus talked about authority in an analogy of a strong man (satan) who must be bound before the goods (sickness) can be plundered (removed from your body). He also said what you bind or loose on earth will be bound or loosed in heaven (see Matt. 12:29; 18:18). If you belong to Jesus, in His name you can bind the enemy, pray, and receive. On the other hand, those who aren't His don't have that authority. After disciples healed and cast out demons, a group of seven sons of the Jewish chief priest Sceva also tried to exorcise demons "by the Jesus whom Paul preache[d]" (Acts 19:13-16). A demon replied that he knew Jesus and Paul, but not them. Then the possessed man overpowered all seven; they ran away, naked and wounded. God used this act for unbelievers to get saved and for believers to repent (see Acts 19:17-18). The demonic has great power when you're in his territory without Jesus' authority. By accepting Jesus, you're not only able to employ His name as your authority, but even demons and sickness must obey.

The Blood

Another example of how you have authority is through the blood of Jesus. Biblical references to blood are massive—360 times in the Old Testament. The use of *blood* is *dam*, either animal or human.[6] Because the "life of the flesh *is* in the blood, [spilling of blood] makes atonement for the soul" (Lev. 17:11). Therefore, God chose animal blood as man's substitute sacrifice to cover sin and make atonement for his soul. That creature's life was in the blood, so its blood was spilled as a vicarious sacrifice for those offering it. Without it, man could have no relationship with the Father.[7] Paul alluded to that sacrifice practice delineated in Leviticus when he said all things are cleansed with blood "and without shedding of blood there is no remission" (forgiveness) (Heb. 9:22).

Blood sacrifice was introduced in Genesis, and that requirement continued through Jesus' sacrifice, man's final atonement. Once a year as the high priest sprinkled animal blood on the Mercy Seat, his and others' sins were temporarily covered because the sacrifice satisfied God's judgment (see Heb. 9:7). However, God's Son took on human form to become the definitive sacrifice. Although the high priest was required to sacrifice for his and others' sins regularly, Jesus sacrificed once and for all by offering Himself (see Heb. 7:27). Instead of the system of animal sacrifices, Jesus became the substitute Lamb who suffered, whose blood was shed, and who was slain. His sacrifice, "not with the blood of goats and calves, but with His own blood," atoned for man's sins forever (Heb. 9:12). His blood cleansed man's sins while demonstrating His love for man (see Rev. 1:5).

Not only was blood part of sacrifices, but early on the use of blood showed believers' authority. Moses asked Pharaoh to let the Hebrews leave Egypt, or the last plague would be the death of the firstborn, from men to animals. That curse was to cover the land, so the Hebrews were instructed to place the blood of a lamb above their doors so the death angel passed over them. That blood was their authority that their houses were exempt from the curse (see Exod. 12:13). Though all firstborn in Egypt were killed, the Lord's children with the blood over their doors were saved. Jesus' blood is now the protection above your door. The practice of anointing doors and windows with oil is still powerful and effective. That sign acts as a covenant of protection like God protected

His people in Egypt. You can claim that authority and place the covering over your body, house, family, marriage, everything.

Jesus' blood over your door gives legal authority and access to healing from sickness, your own death angel. Sometimes when I pray, I envision His bloody, costly stripes and see myself putting my finger in one to claim healing. His blood's power makes you overcome "by the blood of the Lamb and by the word [*logos*] of [your] testimony" (see Rev. 12:11). This use of *blood* is *haima*, defined as the "atoning blood of Christ,"[8] which created salvation for your soul and healing for your body. This use of *testimony* is *marturia*, meaning "evidence given...record, report."[9] This definition implies a legal sense—a legal right to testify of healing. When Jesus promised the disciples Holy Spirit would bring power, He said they'd be His witnesses (give testimony) in all the earth (see Acts 1:8). You report and testify about what Jesus did and legally appropriate that healing.

The Father has given everything into Jesus' hands (see John 3:35). After He offered His own blood as a sacrifice, He conferred His authority to us as He sat down "at the right hand of the Power" (the Father) (Mark 14:62). There, Jesus makes intercession with the Father (see Rom. 8:34), and we're raised to sit with Christ in His authority. Seated at the Father's right hand, He exceeds all other powers and "put[s] all things under His feet...[and is] head over all things" (see Eph. 1:20, 22). Because He paid the price with His blood and makes intercession with the Father, through Him you can come "boldly to the throne of grace" (Heb. 4:16) to receive mercy and grace when you need it. Your boldness and confidence comes through Him (see Eph. 3:12). In another reference, Paul says, you have "boldness to enter the Holiest by the blood of Jesus" (Heb. 10:19). The word for *boldly* and *boldness* in these two scriptures is *parrhesia*, which means "assurance—bold...confidence."[10] In yourself, you have no authority; because of His Son's blood, you can boldly and confidently approach the Father and receive your answer.

Covenant

Authority through your blood covenant with God is a difficult concept to understand because the world no longer cherishes faithfulness to one's word. You sign your name as a pledge then pay lawyers to break unbreakable contracts. God deals with man through covenant, sacred and unbreakable. His covenants demonstrate "the relationship between God and his people."[11] God wanted to establish Adam and Eve forever in a perfect world, but they had to obey Him or face consequences. When they fell, they negated that contract. He then provided animal skins to cover their nakedness. This first shedding of blood was the introduction of animal sacrifice (see Gen. 4:4).

God's covenant with Abraham was a precursor of the covenant of grace through Jesus. God sent Abram from his country and father's house with promises of blessings (see Gen. 12:1-2). He later signified that covenant with circumcision, a cutting involving blood, which became the sign of the Old Testament covenant. Abraham was promised that if he followed God's edicts, he'd have innumerable descendants—like the dirt, stars, and sand (see Gen. 13:16; 22:17). In the wilderness, God gave His law of the covenant to Moses and others who were part of those innumerable descendants. Then Moses prepared animals for sacrifice and read the Book of the Covenant to the people before he offered blood. Therefore, the first covenant of Moses' law was dedicated with blood (see Exod. 24:1-8; Heb. 9:18). However, animal sacrifices became insufficient.

God ushered in a new, better, and final covenant with His Son's blood to cover men's sins. This new covenant had been prophesied: "'Behold, the days are coming,' says the Lord, 'when I will make a new covenant with the house of Israel and with the house of Judah'" (Jer. 31:31; Heb. 8:8). Jesus was the Object of that new covenant. At the Last Supper, He foretold of His sacrificial blood when He took His cup and said, "This cup is the new covenant in My blood, which is shed for you" (Luke 22:20). The next day, His stripes became the sign of our new covenant healing. The symbol of the Old Testament covenant was circumcision. Now the sign of the New Testament covenant is communion as you eat the body and drink the blood of Jesus for your covenant meal. Jesus fulfilled the old covenant and ushered in a new one as He became the "Mediator of a better covenant, which was established on better promises" (Heb. 8:6) and the "surety of a better covenant" (Heb. 7:22). We're ministers of this new covenant because of Holy Spirit, who brought life (see 2 Cor. 3:6).

This new covenant of healing has been personal to me when I received miracles during communion four times. The first time I'd found a lump, which was growing. The second time I'd injured my shoulder, was sleeping with it propped up, and couldn't do even simple tasks like buckling my seatbelt. The last two times my doctor had given me bad reports. Each time, at Wednesday night communion service as we partook of the emblems, I held mine up to the Lord and declared, "The meal that heals!" The first time, the lump disappeared by the next day. The second time I realized my shoulder wasn't hurting later that night as I positioned a pillow beside me in bed to prop up my arm. By rote, I'd left church and buckled my seatbelt with my right hand, a task I'd been unable to do before service. Finally, my reports were miraculously better by the next appointment. God healed as I obeyed His simple unction as a path to victory when I partook of the new covenant meal. Communion itself isn't what heals. It's having faith to call upon His sacrifice and the covenant He ushered in that does the work.

Not every covenant was with blood but was still binding. One example comes with the story of Bartimaeus when he cried out to Jesus. Mark says after He heard the shrieks, Jesus "stood still" (Mark 10:49). Both *stood* and *still* are the same Greek word, *histemi,* having several meanings including "covenant, establish."[12] When Bartimaeus first called out, he asked for mercy from the Son of David, who was a covenant man. He covenanted several times with Jonathan (see 1 Sam. 18:3, for example).

God also made a covenant with David for future generations (see Ps. 89:2-3). Healing is your covenant established in the heavenlies through His mercy and faithfulness. As Jesus stands still to listen to your needs, He establishes a heavenly covenant, but that's not your only healing covenant from the Lord. Though also not with blood, God gave a healing covenant at Marah after the Red Sea (see Exod. 15:22-26). Jesus covenanted with you through bloody stripes on His back, hands, feet, and head from the crown of thorns. Then He paid with His life. As soldiers pierced His side, blood and water flowed forth (see John 19:34). Water generally symbolizes Holy Spirit. His divinity was mixed with His humanity. After Jesus arose, Holy Spirit arrived to dwell within your human body. Holy Spirit enforces God's covenant to you by His power. Healing's already promised and delivered through grace as you receive it by faith.

Spilled Blood

The shedding of blood matters much to God, especially the blood of the innocent. Therefore, He says if someone spills another's blood, the offender's blood must also be spilled (see Gen. 9:6). After Cain killed Abel, God told him his "brother's blood crie[d] out to [Him] from the ground" (Gen. 4:10). Imagine! The spilling of innocent blood cries to God, so He exacts vengeance. Uriah was killed because of David's lust for Bathsheba and Uriah's integrity and faithfulness to his men (see 2 Sam. 11:17). David paid a high price for his sin. Joab shed the innocent blood of Abner and Amasa and was later killed by Solomon (see 1 Kings 2:5, 31). After the priest Zechariah spoke against King Joash's idolatry, they stoned him in the temple (see 2 Chron. 24:20-21). Joash was later killed by his servants. Jesus mentioned the power and consequences that fall on those who shed innocent blood: "that on you may come all the righteous blood shed on the earth, from the blood of righteous Abel to the blood of Zechariah" (Matt. 23:35).

The Lord doesn't overlook the righteous blood of Abel, His prophets, His priests, or those who choose the route of integrity. Their inner being cries out to God. If their blood is so important that it moves God, imagine the power of His Son's spilled blood! If the blood of animals' sacrifices and these righteous men called out to God, "How much more shall the blood of Christ, who through the eternal Spirit offered Himself without spot to God, cleanse your conscience from dead works to serve the living God?" (Heb. 9:14). Jesus was the quintessential innocent spilled blood, and His blood still cries out to God. That blood is so precious to the Father that it petitions Him for your needs whenever you assert that authority for healing.

Holy Anger

Jesus' authority was obvious in the temple scene. He'd already come into town riding a donkey. Branches had covered the road; multitudes had spread more branches and clothes and cried hosannas to Him (see Matt. 21:7-9). Then He entered the temple and saw the money changers' tables. Those men had perverted God's commandments by buying and selling sacrifices for a profit. Jesus didn't do what was politically correct and not alienate temple leaders, wealthy because of this practice. Instead, He grew angry at the "den of thieves" (Matt. 21:13). He not only drove those thieves from the temple but overturned the tables and didn't allow anyone else to bring wares through the temple (see Mark 11:15-16). Then, after He'd driven them out, the blind and lame came to Him in the temple and were healed. Religious leaders grew indignant and more resolved to eliminate Him. Has modern religion become unaware of needs because they're more interested in the bottom line? We should get angry at self-serving religion, which lacks integrity, ignores people's needs, and creates a stench in God's nostrils.

Jesus told the multitudes that "from the days of John the Baptist until now the kingdom of heaven suffers violence, and the violent take it by force" (Matt. 11:12). We need to get angry at the enemy of sickness that pervades the world. One day as I prayed for a lady for healing, I saw a vision of Jesus overturning the money-changers' tables. When those people brought evil, ungodly things into that temple, Jesus took authority over what wasn't supposed to be there. This revelation became a profound *rhema* for me as He revealed that our bodies are like that temple. What enters the body's temple illegally needs to come out. Holy anger should rise in you because of the enemy slipping in and stealing your health. Illness may have invaded your temple and taken up residence like it belongs, but it has no right. Don't ignore it but rather take authority over it.

Jesus didn't overlook the trespassing. He marched into the temple and drove out those illegally profiting then brought healing to the house. Whatever has set up housekeeping must obey when the Master cleans house. If you give Him authority over your temple, He can destroy what shouldn't be there. Interlopers *must* leave—cancer cells *must* dissipate, the pancreas *must* produce insulin, depression *must* leave. They aren't the boss of you! Let Him drive out what's intruded into your life and body. Take it by force! It's a matter of attitude—set your jaw, grit your teeth, stomp your foot, and take authority over what's illegally operating in your temple. Order the enemy to cease and desist his operation. Like David said about Goliath, that uncircumcised Philistine of sickness can't defy God's army (see 1 Sam. 17:26). Sickness can't defy God's plan for you! Command your body to be well, and believe it. It can't stay in God's temple.

The idea of compassion, which I'll discuss more fully in another chapter, is linked to holy anger and violence. In our co-authored book, *Your Holy Spirit Arsenal*, my husband says,

> I define compassion as the firstborn of the union of God's
> agape love married to His wrath against satan and what

sin has done to His creation—man. Compassion is a perfect mixture of God's love for us and fury against His enemies.[13]

Compassion is a component of love, but part of that love is wanting others to prosper in all ways. Getting angry at the enemy for the havoc he's wreaked is part of that love. It's time for holy violence that says, "No more!" Satan has illegally set up shop, so he must evacuate the premises. You should take yours and others' health back by force. That means getting angry enough to take authority over the enemy.

Conclusion

Once, at a Holy Spirit conference Wade and I were hosting, Holy Spirit revealed that someone had eye issues. Three ladies stood. As I prayed, I took authority over those eye problems then continued with the service. That day, they all gave testimonies. One said she was able to read without her glasses. Another was healed from chronic itching in her eyes. The final woman was my sister, Becky. She said she'd been to the doctor who found tumors under her eyelids, and the only viable treatment was surgery. Later that day at the conference, Becky raised her hand, with a wonder-filled expression. She'd felt something in the corner of her eye. Thinking it was a clump of mascara, she removed it with her fingernail. However, instead of make-up, it was one of those tumors. The other tumors dropped out later that day. Acting on God's revelation then taking authority made the enemy flee.

Like the centurion, I understand authority because of my former life roles. As a single mother for many years, I was the disciplinarian; my daughters knew when they got the "Mom look," I meant business and they'd better comply. As a teacher I knew when I issued a command, students were obligated to obey because the weight of office was behind me. Through Him, authority and power work in tandem because He's standing behind you. No matter what the enemy throws, His authority prevails. *Exousia* through His name, His word, and His blood allows you to assert covenant rights and authority. By Jesus' costly sacrifice, God's given you both authority and power to appropriate yours and others' healings. His shed blood speaks to the Father, so healing belongs to you. Like the centurion's humility, Jesus loves humility, but a time comes when you must get angry with the enemy for invading your temple.

Questions to Ponder

Answers in the Appendix

1   a.   How did the centurion demonstrate humility?

      b.   Why would Jesus respond to the centurion's love and humility?

      c.   How did the centurion demonstrate Proverbs 27:2?

      d.   What did Cornelius do that made his prayers heard?

      e.   Why does giving touch God's heart?

2   a.   Explain how the centurion understood Jesus' authority from his own life's experiences.

      b.   Tell how Jesus reclaimed earthly authority.

      c.   Fill in the blanks: ___ ___ is for ___—from ___ to ___ to ___ to ___.

      d.   How does the Greek word for *obey* parallel the centurion?

3   a.   Explain *exousia*.

      b.   According to John 14:10, from whom does Jesus have authority?

      c.   What's the difference between the authority of believers and the enemy's power in Matthew 10:1?

      d.   Which is stronger?

4   a.   Give three ways you have authority from the Lord.

      b.   What's the difference between the *logos* and the *rhema*?

      c.   What are ways you can receive *rhema*?

      d.   Jeremiah 23:29 compares God's Word to what two powerful things?

e. In the Parable of the Sower, what four kinds of ground are seeds sown into, and what types of people do those grounds represent?

f. Explain the author's comment: "Many water down God's word to meet their experiences instead of raising their expectations to meet His word."

g. What type of *word* is used in your Ephesians 6 armor?

5 a. How must you ask the Father, and He'll give whatever you ask?

b. Show how Peter and John's Gate Beautiful experience allowed them to demonstrate and declare the authority of Jesus' name.

c. Were they afraid of consequences? Explain.

d. How does the story of Sceva's sons demonstrate the principle of the authority of Jesus' name?

6 a. Why did God require blood for man's sacrifice?

b. How does Jesus' sacrifice differ from animal sacrifices?

c. Hebrews were protected from what by placing blood above their doors in Egypt?

d. What current practice is similar to this?

e. How do the meanings of the words in Revelation 12:11 show your legal right to healing?

f. What does the right hand of God symbolize?

7 a. Explain covenant.

b. Whom did God covenant with in the Old Testament?

c. Explain the new covenant.

d. What's the symbol of the new covenant? Can you think of a time when you were healed while partaking of the "meal that heals"?

e. How does Bartimaeus' story demonstrate covenant rights?

f. What did the blood and water flowing forth from Jesus symbolize?

g. What healing covenants may we can call upon?

8 a. What is spilled blood?

b. Why and how does God respond to that blood?

c. Give one example from this chapter of those who shed innocent blood and why they were killed.

d. Whose blood is the ultimate example?

e. Why does this spilled blood give authority?

9 a. What were the money-changers illegally doing in the temple?

b. How did Jesus respond?

c. Give the author's analogy of turning over the tables and healing.

d. How does compassion use holy anger as a weapon?

DISCUSSION: Which principle from the story of Jesus and the centurion speaks most to you?

Chapter Five

Holy Spirit

HOLY SPIRIT'S GIFTS BRING AMAZING RESULTS WHEN YOU MAKE them part of your life and ministry. One Sunday morning years ago during service, the Lord showed me a hypodermic needle. I didn't understand, but I shared anyway. That didn't apply to anyone at church; but though it may have looked like I'd missed the mark, I'd experienced enough words of knowledge and wisdom to know God had a plan. Finding out what didn't take long. Our pastor and a group of other ladies were at lunch after service when one went into the restroom. There, a restaurant employee was tying a trash bag and crying from severe tendinitis pain. Her treatment required cortisone injections. Remembering the word from that morning, the lady from church went and got the others. Our pastor, a prolific operator in the gifts, received a word of knowledge to rebuke the spirit of neuropathy. After they finished praying there in the restroom, this afflicted lady rejoiced because she was pain-free for the first time in a long while.

Holy Spirit's gifts are real and vital. However, in today's church, the subject of Holy Spirit brings great disagreement. Though most believe in the Father, Son, and Holy Spirit, their roles are debated. Sadly for some, Holy Spirit has been relegated to barely more than a name on the Trinity letterhead. Others, however, cherish and seek His fullness. After you're infilled with the Spirit, He daily leads, guides, directs, comforts—His roles and wonders are limitless. He has much wealth and power to contribute to your life, and the gifts are essential in healings. For miracles and healing, Holy Spirit has indescribable power.

What Did Jesus Do?

Jesus was on His way with a father to heal his dying daughter. Then, His mission was interrupted by another assignment. Because a large crowd had assembled to see Him, no one had noticed an unremarkable woman edging toward Him as He inched through the throng to bring life back to the girl (see Matt. 9:20-22; Mark 5:25-34; Luke 8:43-48). This desperate woman greatly needed His healing touch. For twelve years, she'd had an issue ("flow" in Luke) with her blood. She'd gone through many doctors' procedures; had spent all her money; but had grown worse (in Mark), not better. She needed an answer for her hopeless situation because all those years, nothing had worked. Now that Jesus traveled down that crowded street, circumstances would change.

She'd probably heard stories about this gentle Carpenter or had watched firsthand as His healing gift had blessed multitudes, so she drew closer. Because her bleeding was probably menstruation, she was considered unclean; that may have accounted for her secretive approach although many factors could have discouraged her. Somehow the woman knew Jesus had the answer that had eluded doctors, if only she could touch Him, even His robe. She guardedly pressed into the massive crowd surrounding Him, approached from behind, reached toward Him, and "touched the hem of His garment" (Matt. 9:20). She took hold and wasn't disappointed. After that touch, she immediately felt power go into her body, the blood flow stopped, and she knew by her body's response that she was healed (see Mark 5:29).

She wasn't the only one who felt something. Jesus also experienced a sensation as an exchange of power went from Him into her. Matthew says He turned immediately, saw her, and told her she was healed because of her faith (see Matt. 9:22). Mark says Jesus perceived power leaving His body and asked who had touched Him or His clothes. Because He was inundated by the large crowd, that seemed like a silly question. Disciples confirmed they hadn't, and Peter wondered why He'd ask that when such crowded circumstances made human contact likely. But Jesus insisted, "Somebody touched Me, for I perceived power going out from Me" (Luke 8:46). He spotted the recipient. After she knew she'd been exposed, she was fearful because of the miracle (see Mark 5:33), perhaps when attention fell on her. She reverently dropped to her knees before Him, confessed in front of everyone, and told of her healing (see Luke 8:47). He said to be of good cheer and to go in peace because her faith had made her whole.

The Power of His Touch

Jesus was filled with Holy Spirit after John baptized Him and before His wilderness experience (see Luke 3:22; 4:1). Operating in that power, He was such a Healer, that He healed on His way to heal. He healed without being asked to heal. He healed when He needed to ask whom He healed. Doesn't that thrill you? Healing anointing permeated His garment, like it later would saturate Peter's shadow or clothing that had touched Paul's body. Can you step into the realm where He uses even what touches you to address another's needs? Whether the touch is from His nail-scarred hands or your touch to His hem, Jesus wants to touch and heal you. His touch healed multitudes—Peter's mother-in-law's fever, blind eyes, severed ears, mute tongues (see Matt. 14:14; 8:15; 9:29; Luke 22:51; Mark

7:33). His touch was so sought after that, at other times, all were healed as throngs gathered to touch Him or carried others for His touch (see Mark 3:10; 6:56).

Jesus' touch was power, even when initiated by another and not from His hands. The garment the desperate woman touched wasn't fancy and likely stained and frayed from His travels on dusty Middle Eastern roads. His hem's fringe wasn't remarkable either, but desperation draws you to touch the Master, even if it's just His ordinary robe. Her touch to Him used the same word as His touching others, *haptomai,* meaning "to attach oneself to."[1] Whether you touch Jesus or He touches you, He *haptomais* you and creates healing surety as His power attaches to and flows into you. Imagine! That touch from those rough Carpenter's hands or to His battered hem attaches itself to you as healing permeates your body and grips you like Velcro. As the lady reached toward Him that day, I don't think she gingerly extended her fingers His way. With the excitement that came with finally having Hope in front of her, she probably expectantly thrust her hand toward Him and grabbed firmly yet briefly on to her long-awaited Answer. Touching Him exceeded all her imagination. His touch now through your human hands can bring those same results.

Going Boldly to Jesus

Jesus operated in Holy Spirit's power and wants you to assert your faith by boldly approaching Him. Many spend exorbitant amounts and deplete funds to address health issues only to come away with afflictions still plaguing them and growing worse. For more than a decade, this woman had entrusted her care to doctors, but she worsened. Doesn't that sound familiar? She'd grown desperate, so she boldly approached the Lord despite what could have held her back. Observing religious rules of the unclean may have stopped her. Feeling shame had probably become her character. Giving up and continuing in the sickness and poverty with which she'd grown familiar might have been easier. Fighting that crowd may have been daunting, and some who knew her problem could have called out negative comments. She wasn't dissuaded from advancing toward Him, though she humbly lowered herself to approach at His feet. Even with incurable ailments, the impossible is where Jesus does His best work; your impossibilities are His realities.

She was motivated to reach Him because she'd heard about His miracles and uttered, "If only I may touch His clothes, I shall be made well" (Mark 5:28). That drive, determination, and faith culminated in her healing. You, too, should approach Jesus boldly and unashamedly. Like James says about wisdom, as you come to Him, He "gives to all liberally and without reproach" (James 1:5). True wisdom is knowing where to go for your answer, then understanding He wants to heal you, coming to Him unashamedly, and worshiping Him. He didn't deride her audacity for touching Him or scold her for invading His space and stealing power, nor will He rebuke you. Instead, He credited her tenacity and faith, which brought the miracle into the realm of completion. Like that faith produced an end to her bleeding and gave peace (see Luke 8:48), He heals your mind and body and brings peace when you come to Him, too.

Gifts of Holy Spirit

Holy Spirit has many roles—Helper and Teacher (see John 14:26), Prophet (see 2 Pet. 1:21), Revealer (see 1 Cor. 2:12-16), Creator of Signs and Wonders (see Rom. 15:19), Consuming Fire (see Luke 3:16), Comforter (see John 14:16 KJV), Counselor (see Isa. 11:2), and others. Because of Jesus' finished work, "if the Spirit of Him who raised Jesus from the dead dwells in you, He who raised Christ from the dead will also give life to your mortal bodies through His Spirit who dwells in you" (Rom. 8:11). If Holy Spirit raised Jesus, you can count on healing and life for your body, too, because of Holy Spirit. Part of His finished work is healing, and Holy Spirit is the conduit. Disciples had seen Holy Spirit's operation during the time they associated with Jesus because He'd been infilled when Holy Spirit had descended upon Him as a dove. At that time John had prophesied that Jesus would baptize with Holy Ghost and fire (see Luke 3:22, 16). After He arose, Jesus told disciples to wait in Jerusalem until they became filled with power from heaven (see Luke 24:49). That power pervaded the house as a mighty wind came, and tongues of fire sat on them to activate Holy Spirit within them (see Acts 2:2-4). After that, disciples had both Jesus' authority and Holy Spirit's power to perform signs and wonders.

While Jesus was on earth, Holy Spirit dwelt *with* disciples. Now, He dwells *in* us (see John 14:17). Jesus' death and resurrection brought salvation and healing while ushering in Holy Spirit and His gifts (see 1 Cor. 12:8-10). These gifts are discussed more fully in our co-authored book, *Your Holy Spirit Arsenal*. The gifts are available to Spirit-filled believers and crucial for an overcomer. Although they're divided into three categories—revelation, speaking, and power—none of the gifts operate in a vacuum but rather in tandem with each other, especially where healing's concerned. Although miracles and healings are power gifts, revelation and speaking gifts are also helpful in healing because they partner with power gifts to make healing manifest. Holy Spirit's power gifts were part of this lady's miracle.

Revelation Gifts

Revelation gifts are often teamed with speaking and power gifts to initiate healing. Revelation gifts—words of wisdom, words of knowledge, and discernment of spirits—are crucial because they let you know past, current, or future events or situations. Operating proficiently in the gifts is a process of growing through experience. Holy Spirit reveals in many ways, usually through unctions, dreams, visions, or circumstances. Words of wisdom have a two-fold purpose. First, they give supernatural wisdom and understanding about situations, what God's saying, and applying that revelation. Second, they're given to alert you about future events. Because the enemy's constantly trying to ensnare you, these revelations allow you to be a diligent and obedient watcher. A wonderful scripture tells how words of wisdom work: "in vain the net is spread in the sight of any bird" (Prov. 1:17). I love this picture. When the Lord gives revelation, and you (the bird) know you'll be attacked by the enemy's net, you can avoid it. Because that word of wisdom alerted you in advance, the net is set "in vain." Snares could be varied—sinful desires, physical attacks, under-handed relationships, decisions that may derail you. They may also be people whom the enemy uses to attack you. Satan attempts to lull you to sleep then sneaks in, but a word of wisdom alerts you.

Discernment of spirits informs you about a person's intentions, good or bad. You can visualize beyond what the human eye sees because Holy Spirit recognizes the heart's motives. Because He knows, use discernment and test the spirits (see Prov. 16:2; 1 John 4:1), even when someone offers to pray for you or claims to have a prophetic word. By this gift you can know whether words or people come in Holy Spirit, flesh, or evil spirits. Putting your hands on someone or that person laying hands on you can transfer good or bad things. Operating in discernment of spirits allows you to know who should touch you or upon whom you should or shouldn't lay your hands (see 1 Tim. 5:22). Trust that discernment. Many Spirit-filled Christians operate in this gift but question when it stirs inside them with an "uh-uh" about someone or something. Believe Holy Spirit and His yes or no nudges, which validate or warn about a person or situation. That tugging might also be God wanting you to intercede for another. Once, I was going through a great trial and felt very alone. Later that week, five people contacted me and said they'd been praying because I was on their hearts. Because they listened and prayed, I found great peace during my storm.

Words of Knowledge

Words of knowledge focus on past or present events or situations in your or others' lives. Of all the revelation gifts, words of knowledge are most closely aligned with healing. Though miracles and healings are power gifts, words of knowledge often initiate them. When a word of knowledge is revealed, an anointing is present for someone to receive healing. Although God's constantly in the healing business, if Holy Spirit spotlights a specific need, an angel brings an anointing for that particular ailment. I compare this to the angel troubling the water so healing could occur (see John 5:2-9). After someone responds, healings come because Holy Spirit spoke, a person voiced that word of knowledge, another claimed it as his/her *rhema*, then he/she acted. Knowing it's going to happen and acting on it triggers the power gift of faith. We've come to say, "What He reveals, He heals" because healings or miracles occur automatically.

We've experienced hundreds of words of knowledge resulting in healing. One night Wade was preaching when I had a word of knowledge about someone's hip. Wide-eyed, a woman raised her hand. Her young daughter had hip problems because one leg was substantially shorter than the other; their doctor was ordering elevated shoes. This mother brought her daughter forward for prayer. I asked the girl to lean against the back of a chair while I perched on the floor in front of her and held her extended legs. I told Wade that one was about an inch shorter.

"No!" the girl corrected, her tiny fingers sticking her long, red hair behind her ear. "It's seven-eighths of an inch." I smiled and apologized. While her small ankles rested in my hands, several gathered around to watch or help pray. Suddenly, I felt one leg move. When I opened my eyes, both were the same length. With eyes wide and staring at her feet, she told me she'd felt something turn in her hip as her leg moved. She stood up and strutted around, nothing wrong with either her leg or hip. Onlookers reacted similarly to what usually happens—wide-eyed expressions as they heard the praise report or actually saw that leg shoot out. Though people are often in disbelief, they have no other explanation except the miraculous.

Another time in a service, I felt a sensation on the side of my face and into my eye and ear. Crying, one lady stood up. Laying her hand on her face, she said a tumor was growing and making her face and ear tingle. She'd come that night for prayer because surgery was the doctor's only answer. God touched her. A few years later, this same lady attended a conference where I spoke. In the Spirit I saw a fungus growing. She tilted her head, pursed her eyebrows, and said she didn't know what it could be. However, she realized how words of knowledge work, so we prayed and believed. A few weeks later she messaged me that after that day, her dentist had discovered a tooth fungus. God intervened, and she didn't lose her teeth. Words of knowledge are a powerful and sure Holy Spirit tool.

Speaking Gifts

Speaking gifts—prophecy, tongues, and interpretation of tongues—are also powerful in healing. After receiving a word from the Lord, you speak it, and it becomes a prophetic word. Because everyone is human, anyone is susceptible to giving false words, even those you hold in high esteem. That's when discernment about others is crucial, but also in checking yourself regularly to assess your own life and motivations. Once King Saul "prophesied" (see 1 Sam. 18:10). As straightforward as that sounds, this statement is troubling. As he was prophesying, he was under the influence of evil spirits. In his heart, he held envy, anger, suspicion, displeasure, unforgiveness, and murder. In his hand, he held a spear with which to kill David and tried twice while they were together (see 1 Sam. 18:8-11). How can you accurately speak God's words and heart of love with wicked things inside you? How can your "prophetic" words demonstrate His heart when yours is full of ugliness, including murder—to reputations, character, prophetic integrity? True words from God are given in love, and your heart must employ a love stance. Even when God gives a hard word, He does that with His heart of love.

These prophetic words are often the result of tongues. Tongues, together with interpretation of tongues, equals prophecy. Because many are confused by these, Paul gives guidelines for tongues and prophecy in an assembly (see 1 Cor. 14:26-40). However, tongues and prophecy are also given privately, as Holy Spirit moves upon you to speak a word to another. Often, that prophetic word is so strong it comes upon you like a fire, and you have to speak it forth like Jeremiah (see Jer. 20:9). When you do, it's authoritative and powerful. But tongues in an assembly aren't the only type of tongues available to Spirit-filled believers.

Prayer Language

When Paul lists the speaking gifts, he uses tongues plurally—"different kinds of tongues" (1 Cor. 12:10). The second type is prayer language. As powerful as words of knowledge are to healing, so are tongues as a prayer language, or praying in the Spirit (see Eph. 6:18). Paul explains that when he prays in tongues his spirit prays though his mind doesn't understand what he's praying (see 1 Cor. 14:14). This type of tongues is different from tongues in an assembly because you don't need to interpret as this doesn't necessarily lead to prophecy. It's often not while you're in a group but rather when you're alone. It's a powerful weapon as you war for healing or anything else you need. As you pray in His language, you can use both His power and the authority of Jesus' name. You may never know what you said, but He does. As you pray or sing in Holy Spirit's language, He directs you about what you should intercede for or don't understand (see Rom. 8:26). Often, you aren't aware of how to pray—doctors can't find what's wrong, your spouse is acting strangely toward you. You don't know everything, even about your own life or body. That's why Holy Spirit's language directs your prayers (see 1 Cor. 2:11). I like for people to pray for me in tongues because their knowledge is limited, and Holy Spirit's is limitless. When I pray for others' healing, I often pray in tongues until He reveals a specific direction so I can then pray in English.

One week, I was part of the Sunday morning ministry team when Ashley came seeking prayer and responded to my invitation to be infilled by Holy Spirit. As her prayer language came, she received the largest dose of Holy Spirit I'd ever seen anyone receive. She collapsed on the chair behind her and was trembling, hooting, and stammering vociferously. The next week another lady in the prayer line received her Holy Ghost mugging (as my husband calls it). Then, the third person in two weeks was baptized in Holy Spirit. As I prayed for each lady, God whispered the same message to me—"How beautiful is the language of Holy Spirit!" I've been around speaking in tongues my whole life and have been Spirit-filled since childhood but never thought of that language in those terms. The beauty of those Holy Spirit-inspired words changes much.

Power Gifts

The speaking and revelation gifts have a purpose, yet they are also often initiators of healings and miracles as they work in conjunction with power gifts—the gift of faith, gifts of healings, and working of miracles. They're part of Holy Spirit's healing arsenal because, by their very names, they hold inherent healing power. As you approach the Lord for your or another's healing, that healing must occur because you come in the confidence and authority of Jesus and the extraordinary *dunamis* power of Holy Spirit. The plural names—gifts of healings and working of miracles—indicate that more than one way exists to receive healings and miracles. That's accomplished as you apply Jesus' blood, use your faith formula from the Word, or receive a word through Holy Spirit's revelation and speaking gifts.

The gift of faith is a power gift different from faith as a result of knowing the Word or applying the faith process. It works with the healings and miracles gifts to create assurance that your answer will happen. I've heard this distinction described as the difference between "I think" or "It is written." As the gift of faith arises, a *surety* happens—you know the miracle, healing, or deliverance will certainly occur. You just know it. My mother operated prolifically in the gift of faith. Whenever the Lord deposited that gift in her, she'd set her jaw and get a determined look my family knew well. The gift of faith assured her many times that God would heal—when doctors predicted my sister would die young of a heart condition, my brother's finger was cut off and Mom put it back on with a Band-Aid, and I was healed from smallpox and developed a natural immunity. I feel that same stubbornness when that gift settles into my spirit. After it's deposited, no matter what circumstances seem to be, that gift of faith creates an it's-gonna-happen reality. Through the gift of faith, no matter how things appear, *it's done.*

Dunamis

Christians have unlimited power available through Holy Spirit, but most don't understand that power or apply it to healing. In my last chapter, I discussed how *exousia* heals through Jesus' name. *Dunamis* is the other type of power, which emanates from Holy Spirit. When Jesus felt power leave His body and go into the woman's (see Luke 8:46), that power was *dunamis*, meaning "might, great force, great ability, strength."[2] He spoke of *dunamis*, saying, "But you shall receive power [*dunamis*] when the Holy Spirit has come upon you" (Acts 1:8). Stephen was described as being "full of faith and power [*dunamis*]" (Acts 6:8) as he performed signs and wonders. As Holy Spirit uses you for healing, you tap into *dunamis*.

Though they're different types of power, both *exousia* and *dunamis* can heal. My husband uses an analogy about a sheriff's role to show the difference between the two. Authority is his badge, which commands respect and obedience because of his office. As his representatives, even his deputies' authority must be acknowledged, or consequences occur. Without that badge, the sheriff has no authority; by wearing it, he must be respected and obeyed. That's *exousia*. *Dunamis* is the sheriff's gun, which can whip through the toughest situation and defeat an enemy without a single word. A gun's power complements and lends force to the sheriff's authority. Similarly, *dunamis* backs up authority. *Exousia* authority stops the enemy in his tracks; Holy Spirit's *dunamis* power destroys him.

Dunamis is the power to which Jesus alluded as He instructed disciples to wait because once they were infilled, that power would be how they would accomplish His promise to do greater works. Jesus referred to it in the story of the lady with the issue of blood when He told Peter "Somebody touched Me, for I perceived power [*dunamis*] going out from Me" (Luke 8:46). Like He felt power leave with the woman's touch, *dunamis* goes from one Source (Holy Spirit working through Spirit-filled believers) into another to accomplish whatever needs to be done. *Dunamis* is transformer power that heals even if you touch a robe's hem, a cut-up apron, or the shadow of someone operating in it. Like Jesus perceived power going from Him, as Holy Spirit's power flows into another, you can tangibly feel that leave your body.

The Lord once told me He'd use me as an extension cord to hook up to a Source and let that power surge into another person. As His might streamed into others through me, I was connected to Holy Spirit as *dunamis* flowed through me to accomplish what was needed. It pours into others as substantial, infusing power or "virtue" (see Luke 8:46 KJV). When I operate in this, I feel significant power in my body. As God uses me for healing, something literally leaves me, and I become the conduit to infuse *dunamis* into someone else's body. I take another's hand, and he/she usually feels that power enter while I feel it leave. As it penetrates, people experience various sensations like heat, pulsations, or electricity. Once, Wade and I visited the hospital room of a lady in great pain after suffering a heart episode. As I took her hands for *dunamis* to flow into her, she felt electricity surge into her hands, up her arms, and into her chest, like her heart had been shocked. The next day we received word she'd been released, instead of the long hospital stay doctors had anticipated.

The lady with the issue of blood's healing wasn't the only one who experienced the *dunamis* power of touching Jesus. In Genessaret, people brought the sick from surrounding regions and begged to be healed by touching His clothes. All who touched them were healed (see Matt 14:34-36). Another time, Jesus and His disciples healed and delivered the sick when a "multitude sought to touch Him, for power [*dunamis*] went out from Him and healed them all" (Luke 6:17-19). *Dunamis* can be transferred by His touch or by your touch to Him for others or your own needs; when it enters, it does what the anointing comes to accomplish. *Dunamis* brings results.

The Anointing

Like in the story about the man being let down from the roof, healing power often permeates a place. That's the anointing. Although many use the word *anointing*, they often don't understand its meaning. The anointing is Holy Spirit's ability that comes upon you to enable you to do many things—sermons, worship, writing, singing, praying. He plants His ability to accomplish what He wants, when He wants. I think of the anointing like adrenaline. You have it in you all the time, but when a dire need arises—a child is trapped beneath a car—it escalates to allow you to perform feats you couldn't ordinarily do. Likewise, a human can't heal another or sing a song that draws the lost unless Holy Spirit enables him/her with His anointing. Once Peter was standing before the Sanhedrin. He'd been asked to explain to them in whose authority he and John had healed at the Gate Beautiful. As he began to speak, Holy Spirit arose in Peter (see Acts 4:8). That was the anointing, which enabled him to speak God's words.

Jesus healed because He was anointed through Holy Spirit. As He declared His earthly assignment, He explained that His Holy Spirit-authored anointing enabled Him to do many mighty works:

> *The Spirit of the Lord is upon Me, because He has anointed Me to preach the gospel to the poor; He has sent Me to heal the brokenhearted, to proclaim liberty to the captives and recovery of sight to the blind, to set at liberty those who are oppressed; to proclaim the acceptable year of the Lord* (Luke 4:18-19).

In this passage, *anointed* is *chrio*, "to smear or rub with oil...to consecrate to an office or relig. service."[3] That definition reminds me of the instruction to anoint others literally with oil, representing healing anointing (see James 5:14). Like you anoint with oil, Holy Spirit anointed Jesus for important jobs—to heal emotionally and physically, bring freedom from sin, deliver, and preach the gospel. Those are your assignments, too, which you can accomplish as Holy Spirit enables you. That anointing lives in you (see 1 John 2:27), and its power helps you accomplish His purpose. As each situation arises, He sends fresh anointing to complete what He pleases. As operators in Holy Spirit's gifts, "you have an anointing from the Holy One, and you know all things" (1 John 2:20). In this scripture, the word for *anointing* is similar to *chrio* but adds something else. *Chrisma* means "an ungent or smearing...the spec. endowment...of the Holy Spirit."[4] He endows you with specific ability as He smears His anointing upon you to "know all things" about which you'd otherwise know nothing.

The anointing is living; that seed within you activates when Holy Spirit needs to use you as His hands. It accompanies healing both to know and bring about the *all things* Jesus proclaimed. It comes upon people differently, often tangibly. Healing evangelist William Branham felt his hand vibrate or an angel walk beside him when he knew healing anointing was present. Until he felt that, he didn't minister because without the anointing, he could do nothing. My husband looks into a person's eyes or hears him/her speak a word, and that sparks something in him. Then he ministers in the anointing. He feels strength in his body while operating in it; after it leaves, he feels exhausted. For me, I sense the anointing through a tingling on my arms, oil on my hands, a breeze wafting in, or a pain where I'm to pray. At times when I see a vision or speak prophetically, I feel anointing rise up in me to pronounce Holy Spirit's revelations authoritatively. The anointing comes differently for every person and situation and always for a purpose.

Receiving Others' Words

When Holy Spirit reveals a need, part of that word's fulfillment lies in how it's received. People don't accept for many reasons, from envy to not wanting a hard word for them to be true. My example of the lady who didn't dismiss the word about the fungus shows how you should receive. If you don't understand what the word means, you should still consider and weigh it because healing is dependent upon how you receive. Accepting the prayer or word of knowledge creates a healing pathway for God to perform that miracle, but you must act on that by demonstrating your faith. That acting could include coming forward, acknowledging, believing, and voicing that your healing is complete. Our pastor once said, "The anointing you respect is the anointing you attract." That's a good thing to remember with healing.

Some prophetic words may seem confusing or silly, even laughable; but God cares about everything concerning you, whether godliness or life (see 2 Pet. 1:3). Once during a service, the Lord told me, "Belly buttons." People giggled until several in that small group had belly button issues. Another time, God gave a word of knowledge about knuckles. As unimportant as that sounded, Willy knew its significance. Because of his knuckles, he hadn't been able to move his fingers that morning, and it had affected him at work. That night, he was instantly healed. Another time, the Lord also spoke to me about knots on the head, which, of course, my pastor husband twisted to "knot-heads." Several people responded. One lady had been involved in a tractor accident years before and had tolerated that tender knot. By the end of the week, her bump was nearly gone and eventually disappeared. Two other ladies stood in for their husbands, whose knots on their heads also disappeared. If belly buttons, knuckles, and knot-heads are important to God, think of how He longs to heal your direst need. God sometimes chooses to do things in a way that seems foolish, but how that foolishness matters!

Another thing we encounter isn't that people think something is foolish, but they don't understand how Holy Spirit heals. That happened one night when God spoke to me about someone's shoulder. A lady in the back had never seen words of knowledge operate but raised her hand when I perfectly described her painful ailment of thirty years. As I laid my hands on her shoulder and power infused into her, pain left. After the service, she told me her shoulders were still hot. If people don't receive your words, don't get discouraged. Paul must've experienced prior rejection of his words because he commented about receivers at Thessalonica: "For this reason we also thank God without ceasing, because when you received the word of God which you heard from us, you welcomed it not as the word of men, but as it is in truth, the word of God" (1 Thess. 2:13). This scripture implies he'd been rejected elsewhere, but he persisted in speaking God's words.

The Bereans didn't dismiss a word but received it gladly then searched scriptures themselves (see Acts 17:11). That investigation is important because words must witness with Scripture and your spirit. Most words will be right, but using discernment is important in determining the word's accuracy. You may be surprised at who has a right-on word for you, so don't automatically negatively judge the giver. We wouldn't necessarily choose people God uses. Some words from others may even be incorrect on some level but not because of evil or fleshly motives. Holy Spirit uses regular people, every one human and imperfect, so an incomplete or misinterpreted word will happen at times. Paul says, "We see through a glass, darkly" (see 1 Cor. 13:12) because our humanness impacts spiritual discernment. Don't dismiss a flawed word automatically as a false word.

I experienced this personally through imperfect words from an imperfect operator in the gifts, but they brought perfect healing. Twice, Herb gave words of knowledge about serious ailments in my body, but neither was perfectly phrased. Once, he stated something was wrong with my head when I'd been having pain at the bottom of my eye socket and felt a growth there. Another time, he said my finger needed healing when it was my toe. I'd already seen a doctor who was sending me for more tests to determine if the problem was melanoma. I knew Herb could hear from the Lord, he lived right, and he always spoke in humility and love. Both times, I received his flawed words because he was like the rest of us, learning with each new revelation. Both times, I was healed, and pain and symptoms never returned.

After Saul had been blinded on the Road to Damascus, he saw a vision of Ananias putting his hand on him so his sight would be restored. Simultaneously, God showed Ananias that he should minister to Saul. Both men had been moved on by Holy Spirit's revelation and speaking gifts to bring about the power gift for Saul's miracle. Yet, both had reasons not to trust each other because of their histories. Saul had hated Christians in the past, and Ananias knew Saul might kill him because he'd heard stories of Saul's persecutions and martyrdoms. Both, however, were obedient and received the other's words. As a result, scales fell from Saul's eyes (see Acts 9:12, 18), and Ananias helped usher him into the wonderful ministry that still guides the church, especially about Holy Spirit's gifts. Even then, though, when Saul began to preach, people still judged him and were suspicious of him. Despite this, he continued and grew (see Acts 9:20-22).

Reacting to rejection can derail you as you learn to move in the Spirit, but Jesus is your example. People who knew Him personally didn't receive His words either. Even His own people thought He was crazy; some ran Him out of the city and planned to throw Him from a cliff (see Mark 3:21; Luke 4:29). After being misjudged and rejected by His former friends and neighbors, He declared that prophets have honor, but not in their own country. As a result, He couldn't do much in their midst (see Mark 6:4-5). How sad that *they* lost out by questioning Holy Spirit's ability at work in Him. Prophetic words from God are pearls. When people trample on those, remember who gave them and work more diligently with your gifts to help those who do cherish them (see Matt. 7:6). Jesus did. Receiving is truly a blessing.

Conclusion

A while back, Wade and I were eating out. While waiting for the bill, I got a pain in my forearm. Knowing how my gift of words of knowledge works, I asked Wade then our server if either suffered with that. When I pointed, the waiter confirmed he had tumors growing on his arm at that spot. We prayed for him at the table. Although we never saw him again or found out about his healing, I know Holy Spirit had a purpose for that revelation. That night accomplished something we may never hear about; but what He reveals, He heals. I'm sure that young man's life was changed because God knew him.

Many healings happen through Holy Spirit's revelation, speaking, and power gifts, which heal and draw the lost. If you want to make healing commonplace, you must keep the Father's Spirit in His place.

Because of neglecting Holy Spirit's role, many churches are infertile in the healing realm and lack access to His *dunamis* power. As you boldly go for healing, His powerful touch is accomplished through your touch as you receive Holy Spirit's anointing for yourself and others. You receive as you accept what He has to give, through whomever and however He chooses—prophetic actions, praying in tongues, laying hands on others. Holy Spirit needs to occupy a crucial position in lives.

Questions to Ponder

Answers in the Appendix

1   a.   Give examples of how Jesus and others healed through touching.

     b.   How was His touch for the lady with the issue of blood different from most other times Jesus healed?

     c.   Explain the word *haptomai* and its healing significance.

     d.   How does Jesus touch others now?

2   a.   How does this healing show boldness in coming to Jesus?

     b.   What were things she overcame to approach Him?

     c.   How did her words as she touched Jesus demonstrate faith?

     d.   Fill in the blanks: ___ ___ is knowing where to go for your ___, then ___ He wants to ___ you, coming to Him ___, and ___ Him.

3   a.   What are some of Holy Spirit's roles?

     b.   What's the difference between how Holy Spirit operated with men during Jesus' time and now?

     c.   What does the author mean that "none of the gifts operate in a vacuum"?

4   a.   List the revelation gifts.

     b.   Give specific ways to receive words of wisdom and knowledge.

     c.   Give two purposes for words of wisdom.

     d.   Explain how Proverbs 1:17 shows how words of wisdom work.

     e.   What is the gift of discernment?

5   a.   What are words of knowledge?

        b.   Why does the author say they're closely aligned to the healings and miracles gifts?

        c.   Fill in the blanks: "What ___ ___, He ___."

6   a.   List the speaking gifts.

        b.   Tell how King Saul teaches to assess your heart to see if something could negatively impact prophetic words.

        c.   Tongues plus interpretation of tongues equals what?

        d.   Why did Paul give guidelines for tongues and prophecy in an assembly?

7   a.   Explain the difference between tongues in an assembly and prayer language.

        b.   What are advantages to praying in tongues?

        c.   What does the author say is beautiful to the Father?

8   a.   What are power gifts?

        b.   Why are the gifts of healings and working of miracles listed plurally?

        c.   Describe the difference between the gift of faith and faith as a result of following the process from the Word.

9   a.   What kind of power went from Jesus into the lady with the issue of blood?

        b.   That power comes from whom and is defined as what?

        c.   Give the analogy the author uses for the difference between *exousia* and *dunamis* power.

        d.   To what great power does the author compare *dunamis*?

        e.   Describe how *dunamis* flows from one source to another.

10   a.   What's the anointing?

b. In Luke 4:18-19, what does Jesus say He was anointed to do?

c. Holy Spirit's anointing on you empowers you to know what (1 John 2:20)? Can you share a time when that power was on you or another person?

11 a. When someone receives a word from the Lord, what's an important part of that coming to fulfillment?

b. What are reasons some may not receive a word?

c. What reaction should you avoid if people don't receive your words?

d. Explain how the Bereans received.

e. What reasons made Saul and Ananias mistrust one another?

DISCUSSION: Which principle from the story about the woman with issue of blood speaks most to you?

Chapter Six

Healing Tools

GOD USES MANY WAYS TO HEAL. ONCE, THE LORD LED ME TO PRAY with another ministry partner over a prayer cloth for a man with such bad diabetes that whenever he walked even short distances, his feet and toes would swell, crack, and seep. I took the cloth to him and asked him to put it into his shoe. A few weeks later, his diabetes was better, his feet weren't swollen, and the skin on his toes was healed and smooth. He's now able to walk long distances with no swelling. Another time at a service, the Lord gave a word of knowledge that people needed deliverance from high blood pressure. After several responded, Wade had them come to the altar and line up across the front. As he passed by, many were slain in the Spirit, and God did a work while they lay there. One lady had been on two medications and left that night feeling much better. A man said that for the first time in seventeen years he didn't hear ringing in his ears. Another said she felt peace permeate her body. God accomplishes healings through the use of many tools.

In your home, garage, office, and other places, you have tools to accomplish various tasks. In the kitchen, colanders, knives, cutting boards, and cheese graters all have specific functions. In the garage, hammers, pliers, hoes, and a lawn mower also have unique purposes. My office houses a stapler, computer, printer, paper punch. If you understand how to use varied tools for different needs, your job is successful. Using my knife to drain spaghetti would be problematic. My hammer would be ineffective in mowing grass. I can't staple a document onto my computer. The same concept applies to healing. Holy Spirit has tools to accomplish certain results, and healing is aided by knowing what they are and how to use them. When He reveals His tool, His *rhema* for that situation, healing happens.

What Did Jesus Do?

One day, a multitude had gathered, including a synagogue ruler, Jairus. He approached Jesus because his only child, a twelve-year-old daughter, was dying (she was already dead in Matthew) (see Matt. 9:18-19, 23-25; Mark 5:22-24, 35-43; Luke 8:41-42, 49-56). As Jairus approached the Master, he worshiped Him (fell at His feet in Mark and Luke) and begged Him to come to his house and lay His hand on the girl so she'd be healed (see Luke 8:41). Those words of faith touched Jesus, so He started toward Jairus' home. However, as He and Jairus turned toward the house, the story was interrupted by another healing of the lady with a blood issue.

As He finished that healing, someone told Jairus his daughter had already died, so He shouldn't bother Jesus (in Mark and Luke). In Matthew, Jesus discovered this fact upon going to Jairus' house and encountering professional mourners. Mark and Luke say before they left for the house but after they heard about the death, Jesus told Jairus to "not be afraid; only believe" (Mark 5:36). Then, He stated the daughter was sleeping and not dead. These words made the mourners laugh boisterously in ridicule. That reaction may have been why He put everyone out except His inner circle and the child's parents. He then authoritatively spoke to dead girl. He took her hand and said, "Talitha, cumi...Little girl, I say to you, arise" (Mark 5:41). Immediately she arose and walked. Then, Mark and Luke add two details that sound like Jesus. Though everyone was amazed, in His humble fashion, Jesus asked them not to tell others about the healing (see Mark 5:43). Then, He said to give her something to eat.

Unlikely Seekers

Like many of Jesus' stories, this account provides much insight for how to recognize and apply available healing tools. One lesson is that God uses healings to draw others, and you may be surprised who comes for prayer. Jairus was a synagogue leader, a group that didn't celebrate Jesus' healings or knowledge of Scripture. They hated His disdain of their established, religious ways. They envied His gifts, resented His popularity, and plotted to get rid of Him. Doesn't that sound familiar? Some maliciously malign others' characters to promote themselves. Many earnest believers attend assemblies without an agenda except to help the church and obey God's direction. However, instead of the congregation embracing and welcoming what new arrivals bring to their body, they're talked about, viewed suspiciously, and shunned.

This story is the only biblical reference to Jairus; but as part of the synagogue leadership, he likely felt negatively toward Jesus, disparaged, and persecuted Him in the past. Even if He didn't actively campaign against Him, Jairus probably spoke against Him or didn't feel liberty to acknowledge the truth about his belief in Jesus. Then his world fell apart when his beloved, pre-teen daughter was dying. Though at one time he may have criticized Jesus, he knew in his heart what was real. He didn't go to his religious colleagues who'd been educated about God but had no relationship with Him. He sought Jesus for his answer.

Wade and I see those aspects at work in ministries. When someone operates in the anointing, he/she is a target of envy or persecution from those with self-promoting agendas or who don't understand how the gifts operate. We've heard negative comments about us or others who've sought a deeper Holy Spirit walk and therefore were denigrated by some. However, when these same people needed a dire answer—when their child's or their own lives hung in the balance—like Jairus, they sought those who could touch the throne. I once heard that bank tellers are trained to spot fakes by studying real dollars. Though scoffers may have been part of past gossip and may be again in the future, they're watching and deep down know what's real and who truly operates in power and authority. If someone speaks against you, don't become discouraged about the miraculous path on which the Lord has sent you. Jesus suffered the same types of persecution.

Even those who knew Jesus as the Healer discouraged Jairus' seeking his answer, saying she was already dead and not to trouble the Master (see Mark 5:35). Like Jairus and Bartimaeus, many who were desperate for healing were instructed not to bother Him. Going against popular opinion must have been uncomfortable; but if they'd have listened to naysayers' faulty logic, they would've missed great miracles. He wants you to "bother" Him because He cares about everything involving you. He was concerned enough to make that trip to Jairus' house to heal the girl, but He also cared about her daddy's sorrow and fear at news of her death. He even cared that she just might be hungry. He cares.

Fervent Prayer

Praying fervently is a powerful healing tool. This day with Jairus, Jesus was met by a multitude with great needs, and He performed two of His most renowned miracles. He didn't just show up there and decide He had to pray. That was His lifestyle and should be ours, too:

Is any among you sick? Let him call for the elders of the church, and let them pray. ...And the prayer of faith will save the sick, and the Lord will raise him up...pray one for another, that you may be healed. The effectual fervent prayer of a righteous man avails much (James 5:14-16).

Three times, these verses say prayer heals the sick. I love James' words "effectual fervent prayer." Many forget the fervently and effectively part. I call those "microwave pray-ers"—short and sweet. Some erratically set aside prayer time and multi-task by sandwiching it in on trips to the grocery or the gym. Although those occasions are great for extra prayer, they shouldn't be the primary time you talk to God. You should pray continually (see 1 Thess. 5:17). Fervent prayer accomplishes a lot because He rewards those who seek Him diligently (see Heb. 11:6). It even makes you able to perform resurrections that speak to unbelievers or to those who operate in powerless religions.

Fervent prayer is so important that Jesus told the parable of the persistent widow, who appeared before a judge many times to get justice from her enemy (see Luke 18:1-5). Though at first he turned her down, he ultimately acquiesced, saying, "I will avenge her, lest by her continual coming she weary me" (Luke 18:5). In another parable, Jesus told about a tenacious man who brought a request to his friend and "because of his persistence, [the friend rose and gave] him [what] he need[ed]" (Luke 11:8). If you persevere, God responds. Jesus says, "shall God not avenge His own elect who cry out day and night to Him?" (Luke 18:7). Satan's your enemy who puts anything in your path to assault and discourage you. Through crying out day and night, you touch the Lord, who exacts vengeance for you. Fervent prayer takes you to the Father regularly and intensely until breakthrough comes. Solomon commented about how God responds to persistence: "I love those who love me, and those who seek me diligently will find me" (Prov. 8:17). Do you need to find answers? Unrelenting prayer takes you there.

Because many were desperate and sought Him for healing, Jesus needed time to be alone with His Father, so He "often withdrew into the wilderness and prayed" (Luke 5:16). When you pray, retreat to a solitary place, just you and God. Time alone with the Lord does much to refill and prepare you. Many call that their prayer closet or secret place. When Saul sought to kill David, Jonathan told him to hide in his "secret place" (1 Sam. 19:2). David knew about that place because he often needed his alone time with God. Jesus says you should pray privately in that secret place; as a result, God will openly reward you (see Matt. 6:6). Private prayer time is crucial for healings to occur. Because ministry is physically hard, especially when power goes from your body to another's, you need to be rejuvenated from time to time. Jesus' strength was sapped by healing "an innumerable multitude of people [so massive that] they trampled one another" (Luke 12:1).

Like Jesus, after a time of great ministry, you must replenish what you give out. Prayer renews your spirit, soul, and body so you have more for others. After Jesus came from a great teaching, He healed the leper. Jesus told him not to tell anyone; but he spread the report, and great multitudes came to hear Jesus and be healed. Because of this, He had to stay outside of the city in deserted places (see Mark 1:40-45). He prepared for those healing demands through His solitary time in prayer. At the beginning of His ministry, Jesus needed to choose disciples. Facing such an important decision, He secluded Himself on "the mountain to pray, and continued all night in prayer to God" (Luke 6:12). Continuing alone all night exemplifies fervent prayer.

Another time He had a meeting, which the whole town attended, and He healed and delivered many. Then, He rose early in the morning and prayed in a "solitary place" (Mark 1:35) before Peter and others found Him. Praying early before others have arisen often eliminates distractions that may hinder prayer. In Gethsemane, though He knew about the upcoming ordeal, He prayed so fervently His sweat became as blood (see Luke 22:44). A few days after He'd told His disciples He'd soon be killed, He took His inner circle to the mountain for prayer. There, He prayed so intensely His appearance was altered, and the Transfiguration occurred with Moses and Elijah, both also men of prayer (see Luke 9:29). The importance of this prayer time wasn't just because of this intense glory event. He had to prepare for their descent from the mountain the next day when such a hard deliverance awaited that disciples couldn't exorcise demons.

Even when you know the answer's on the way, fervent prayer is necessary. Elijah knew God would be faithful to His promises, but he still climbed the mountain of prayer—to start the drought, to initiate the sacrifice, and then to stop the drought after three and a half years. His fervent prayers were so powerful they affected nature. Intense prayer on the mountain made the sacrifice be consumed and brought the rain cloud on the horizon (see 1 Kings 18:36, 42; James 5:17-18; 1 Kings 18:44). In addition, Elijah performed a supernatural feat of running twenty-five miles, overcoming great depression, and traveling on a forty-day trip to the mountain of God (see 1 Kings 19). Prayer brings answers and makes you ready for whatever comes next. Though the Lord already knows before you ask (see Matt. 6:8), He wants you to bring your fervent petitions to Him.

Do Not Fear

The healing tool of faith is negated by its opposite—fear. Desperation often leads you to beg the Lord to bring healing to your house, and that act of brokenness isn't lost on the Great Healer. However, desperation can also bring fear. After Jairus' friends told him his daughter had died, Jesus' first words to Jairus were to tell him not to be afraid, but to believe (see Mark 5:36). How like Jesus both to console and instruct a parent who'd received devastating news! He cares for the ailing as well as their loved ones. These instructions give another message. Before healing can come, you must deal with fear.

As a human, He understood Jairus' anguish of loss. However, He had more than sympathy for Jairus. Unlike Jairus' family, friends, and mourners, Jesus had words of life and healing. "Do not be afraid" is still His message. We live in a world of negativity, which permeates our minds with pessimism—*You look sick! Do you feel bad? People never recover from that type of cancer. Ya gotta face reality!* The list goes on. As you receive discouraging reports and react in fear, you change His healing plans. Many places in this book deal with faith and fear because Jesus' ministry demonstrated faith and total confidence in God. When Jesus told Jairus not to fear, He didn't stop at what *not* to do. He also told him what he *should do*—believe. Believing is a tool that works! Healing comes as a result of faith, not fear.

Understanding these dynamics once changed my daughter's destiny. She had a physical problem that necessitated seeing a doctor. The week before her appointment, while I was praying, the Lord spoke, "Don't believe the doctor's report." I knew that message was for her and me. I shared that; but as days passed before her appointment, she forgot. After her appointment, she called, sobbing about a bad report. She'd fallen into the fear trap; I may have too, but God had come before.

I reminded her, "Remember what the Lord said? We're not to believe the report!" When she heard that, tears stopped.

"I forgot, Mom." The rest of our conversation wasn't filled with *oh nos, what ifs,* or details of what the doctor had stated. Her report wasn't in our hands, and the Lord already had it covered. Before day's end, she called me again. The doctor had phoned to say they'd made a mistake, and she was fine. Fear is faith's opposite; they both change things, one for the worse and one for the better. My daughter's report resembled Jairus'—the total opposite of what Jesus said. How often does Jesus' account differ from a doctor's pronouncement? How often do you need to make a conscious choice about which report you'll believe, Jairus' mourners who pronounce death or Jesus who declares life? Remember what He told disciples about how to receive the impossible. You must believe, speak what you believe will happen, and *then* you'll have it. You don't believe *after* you receive. Believe *then* receive (see Mark 11:24).

Breakthrough Tools

One Accord

Some of your daily tools are for simple tasks like a hammer to put a nail into the wall, but others do heavy-duty jobs, like a jackhammer to bust up your sidewalk. When you need great breakthrough, more powerful tools and knowledge of how to apply them are required. I've already discussed Holy Spirit's gifts as an aid for "impossible" healing needs, but others are also available. A powerful breakthrough tool is one accord, which brings amazing results when people go to God in unity. Jesus demonstrated this concept in Jairus' story when He cleared the house. Others in the Bible also put out all or nearly all people before they prayed. The Shunammite son was raised when Elisha was alone in his room (see 2 Kings 4:33). Elijah took the widow of Zarephath's son away from her and went alone to his room to resurrect him (see 1 Kings 17:19). Peter put everyone out when he brought Tabitha to life (see Acts 9:40).

Many reasons may explain why biblical saints made others leave and why you must separate from them. Those who loved the dead person could react in fear and emotional outbursts. Maybe people's taunts (like the mourners), unbelief, lack of focus, negativity, or desire to be an audience and see the show would derail God's plan. Some may lack your type of faith. I've been in services where some were ministering to desperate needs while supposedly mature Christians were zoning out, chatting, or laughing. Sometimes, you should clear the house to make room for healing to come in. Is healing evading you because your personal group is a distraction you still allow in your house and thus disrupt one accord? Jesus told those in Jairus' house to "Make room" because the daughter was sleeping (Matt. 9:24). Mark says that before He departed for Jairus' house, Jesus left everyone except His inner circle, even other disciples (see Mark 5:37). To exclude some from your godly assignments may be uncomfortable, but Jesus was more interested in being about His Father's business than assuaging hurt feelings of disciples who didn't get invited. In ministry as well as daily life, you must be selective concerning associations, even with other ministers. Are you welcoming the Healer in, or is your house filled with people or stuff that keeps Him out?

For Jairus' daughter, "when the crowd was put outside, He went in and took her by the hand" (Matt. 9:25). Jesus didn't start His healing process until He cleared the house of what might derail it. Does that speak to you? Are others' attitudes blocking the Healer from coming in? Before Paul listed the gifts of the Spirit he advised that "everyone who is among you, [should not] think *of himself* more highly than he ought to think, but to think soberly, as God has dealt to each one a measure of faith" (Rom. 12:3). God's given each of His kids this faith measure, but sometimes people forget the unselfish and sober part. The Lord has much for us to do in these latter days, so staying focused and seeking prayer partners of great selflessness, faith, soberness, and one accord helps with intense ministry.

Paul also mentioned that some cause divisions instead of one accord and to "avoid them" (Rom. 16:17). He understood one accord's power personally. He'd been dragged out of the city, stoned, then left for dead (see Acts 14:19-20). Although Luke didn't say he *was* dead, chances are good that he was, after that horrific punishment inflicted upon him. These disciples must have felt sorrow as the man who had taken up the cause of their Master had been so brutally abused. As they gathered in unity around his tattered, broken body, Paul "rose up" (Acts 14:20). Because the miracle they needed was so great whether he was dead or nearly dead, they prayed in one accord. One accord brings much, even resurrections.

Staying in one accord accomplishes great things. When people had built the Tower of Babel, God scattered them because "Indeed the people are one [accord] and they all have one language...nothing that they propose to do will be withheld from them" (Gen. 11:6). If this is true with the ungodly, imagine what Spirit-filled believers can do in one accord. First century believers performed great miracles in one accord. As they gathered in one accord in an upper room, Holy Spirit came down as a mighty wind with tongues of fire, and they became filled with Holy Spirit. People acted in one accord and saw many added to the church (see Acts 2:1-4, 46-47). After Peter and John were released from prison, people rejoiced in one accord, and the place shook. After Ananias and Sapphira were struck down, disciples operated in one accord, and mighty signs, wonders, and salvations occurred (see Acts 4:24, 31; 5:5-14). Something happens in the heavenlies when you're together, for "if two of you agree on earth concerning anything that they ask, it will be done for them by the Father in heaven" (Matt. 18:19). Agreement is important because unity with others forms a powerful alliance that reaches heaven. It's like completing the circuit when starting a car. One accord is a powerful tool.

Travail

Another formidable, yet misunderstood, breakthrough tool is travail, which shatters the unbreakable. As a child I witnessed my mother and others engage frequently in this extreme intercession; yet until I grew older, I didn't know the tremendous force behind it or even what to call it. The Bible compares travail to childbirth (see John 16:21-22) because God uses it to birth answers. Several biblical references describe how it works. As Hannah tarried in the temple, she wanted literally to birth a child. The description of her intense crying speaks of travail because, "in bitterness of soul, [she] prayed to the Lord and wept in anguish" (1 Sam. 1:10), sobbing so hard Eli thought she was drunk (see 1 Sam. 1:14). She wept silently, though travail usually entails loud, boisterous sobs. At times, though, I've felt sobs coming from my being's depths but suppressed the extreme weeping until I could freely cry out to the Lord.

During those times, I could feel travail welling in me and, like Hannah, prayed and cried silently. By the way, Eli's reaction is similar to many who misunderstand this gift. During travail, some may think the travailer has gone crazy or is extremely sad, so they gather around to comfort. However, the travailer should be left alone to complete the process! Breakthrough's needed, and willing vessels are conduits through which it will come to produce a miracle that shatters the unbreakable wall of unanswered prayer. After Eli promised her that God would grant her petition, Hannah stopped crying because she knew breakthrough had come even before the conception or birth occurred (see 1 Sam. 1:17-18). She had faith to get up and go home, confident in God's purpose for her.

Another example of travail and breakthrough is Elijah on the mountain (see 1 Kings 18:41-46). God had shown him how to get fire from heaven to return backsliders to Him. He prayed, and flames descended to consume the sacrifice. Then, when God wanted to birth an end to the drought and a miraculous journey for Elijah to beat the chariots, travail was key. Elijah employed this breakthrough gift as he bowed on the ground on Mt. Carmel in prayer, poised in a childbirth position to burst through for that deluge (see 1 Kings 18:42). Does that speak to you? For big needs, you should use a tool that can end your long-time drought. Travail is that tool to complete your quest to birth the extraordinary—your own Samuels, an end to your drought, or the miraculous becoming reality.

Another example of travail involved Jesus. After He returned to Bethany where two sisters were grieving, He also wept (see John 11:35). I believe His weeping was travail and not just tears of sorrow because

Jesus "groaned in the spirit," was troubled, then wept (John 11:33, 35). This describes travail. Though the interpretation of *groaned* doesn't say the word *travail*, for *spirit*, John uses *pneuma*, which usually refers to Holy Spirit.[1] Paul also uses *groaning* with a Holy Spirit connection: "the Spirit Himself makes intercession for us with groanings which cannot be uttered" (Rom. 8:26). Here, *groanings* is the Greek *stenagmos*, to "murmur, pray inaudibly—with grief."[2] *Inaudibly* describes how, like Hannah, those groans you sometimes hold inside seem like intense grief that will burst forth. When you let them go, they're loud, boisterous, and forceful, issuing from the core. Groans are usually accompanied by ugly sobs—Wade says my travail sounds like a bull moose in distress. Oh, what beauty results from those loud and ugly groans, sobs, and bull-moose howls!

Fasting

Another breakthrough power tool is fasting. While travail often occurs publically while praying for others, fasting is done in privacy and humility (see Matt. 6:17-18). Travail sweeps upon you suddenly like a wave and generally lasts a short time while fasting is done over an extended time as Holy Spirit leads. They both often go hand in hand; but in my experience, travail breaks through the barrier quicker than fasting. That doesn't mean it's less effective as a breakthrough tool. Hannah fasted *and* travailed before receiving her promise. Saul fasted for breakthrough when he was seeking his sight, both physically and spiritually (see Acts 9:9). Elijah's time on the mountain included both travail and fasting. After the sacrifice, while Ahab and others had a great feast, Elijah didn't eat but prayed on the mountain (see 1 Kings 18:41-42). What an awesome time in the Lord he must have had as he used two jackhammer tools—fasting and travail—to change nature and break the drought that had impacted all known nations!

Fasting is usually done privately; but when a group fasts in one accord, it's extremely powerful. Esther called a corporate fast as she approached the king for her nation (see Est. 4:16). She wasn't killed and was able to expose and eliminate her people's enemy. Jehoshaphat's Judah faced an impossible situation of three huge enemy armies; he called a corporate fast. As a result, God not only spoke the M.O., but He brought such profound victory that Jehoshaphat's army gathered spoils three days (see 2 Chron. 20:2-3, 25). After Jonah spoke against Ninevah, the king decreed a corporate fast, which saved their city from destruction (see Jon. 3:7). Fasting, both individually and corporately, should be a tool Christians use regularly. If you need a miracle, fasting opens the realm of the impossible where Jesus works.

Jesus believed in fasting. After being filled with Holy Spirit and before His ministry began, the Spirit led Him into the wilderness to fast and pray for forty days. While in danger of wild beasts and the enemy's temptation, angels ministered to Him (see Mark 1:13). Though His body hungered, His spirit thrived through fasting. I've heard it described this way—when your body fasts, your spirit feasts. When He finished the fast, He returned to His ministry in Holy Spirit's power (see Luke 4:14). Fasting was part of the preparation and power infilling before the most important ministry ever on earth. Like Holy Spirit led Jesus, His leading in your fast is crucial or you shouldn't fast. The key is to fast Holy Spirit's way, and victory comes through obedience coupled with prayer. Fasting is individual between you and God for each fasting occurrence. Let Him show how and how long to fast, and food isn't the only possibility. Sometimes people eat nothing and drink just water and juice, but sometimes Holy Spirit says to fast certain meals or items such as TV, Cokes, your cell phone. I've even heard of people who fasted make-up. Fasting gets your flesh out of the way and allows you to keep your mind off what you'll have for dinner or common activities and distractions. Then you can spend that time in prayer.

Jesus told disciples they couldn't cast out the formidable demons because they hadn't prepared through prayer and fasting (see Mark 9:29). His statements imply that for less dire needs, power tools like travail and fasting are probably unnecessary. However, hard petitions like making rain come or exorcising demons so powerful they can bruise their host should be teamed with extreme power tools. Do you have a need for which you can't get victory? What have you been seeking in the realm of the impossible: A deluge of blessings that breaks your droughts? A birthing of ministry? A resurrection of something seemingly dead? Travail, one accord, and fasting are wondrous, powerful Holy Spirit tools that bring great change.

Conclusion

Healing tools are varied and powerful. One day, a friend texted me about a lady with foster children whose biological father had gotten out of prison and was seeking custody. His history showed that if he regained custody, it wouldn't bode well for the children, so we prayed fervently. That night, he was arrested on a repeat probation violation and couldn't apply any longer. Another time, I felt led to call travailers to come to our home for extreme breakthrough when my friend had been diagnosed with cancer. We went to the Lord in intercession and travailed until we felt breakthrough. She's still cancer-free.

Prayer is a healing tool you should always employ. Praying fervently, regardless of the need, brings answers as God responds to your repeated petitions. That prayer time may be alone with God, but sometimes you need to get with other Christians to pray and fast in one accord. Whether by yourself or with others, prayer truly changes things. As you proceed in faith rather than fear, you're attacking problems in your and others' lives, even people you never thought would seek your prayers. Sometimes your needs will require extreme breakthrough, so Holy Spirit gives powerful tools and weapons that do the job. Be sensitive to His leading, and use those tools He's appropriated for whatever you need. For hard prayer needs, travail, fasting, and one accord break impossibilities, even the elements of nature. God's tools are perfect for every prayer need.

Questions to Ponder

Answers in the Appendix

1 a. Why was it unusual that Jairus sought healing from Jesus?

   b. Why were temple leaders anti-Jesus?

   c. What changed Jairus' mind about coming to Jesus?

   d. How did his coming demonstrate his opinion of the real deal?

   e. Give the analogy about bank tellers.

2 a. What's fervent prayer?

   b. What does Jesus teach in the parables of the persistent widow and the friend?

   c. Why did Jesus often pray in a solitary place?

   d. Give examples of Jesus' fervent prayers.

   e. What did Elijah's fervent prayers accomplish?

3 a. What is faith's opposite?

   b. After Jesus told Jairus not to fear, what did He tell him to do?

   c. Fill in the blanks: "___ ___ can come, you ___ ___ with ___."

   d. How was Jesus' compassion different from the mourners' sympathy? What must you do *before* you receive?

4 a. Explain breakthrough tools.

   b. How is Jairus' story an example of the importance of one accord?

   c. Give reasons others' presence may impede healing.

   d. Jesus didn't begin the healing until after what happened?

e. What two things do you need to watch as you employ your "measure of faith"?

f. Tell the story of Paul's miracle because of one accord.

g. Give New Testament examples of great things that happened as a result of one accord.

5 a. To what does the Bible compare travail?

b. Describe how travail works.

c. How do Elijah's actions on Mt. Carmel exemplify travail?

d. Why does the author think Jesus travailed?

6 a. Although fasting and travail are similar tools, show differences.

b. Give examples of biblical corporate fasts in one accord.

c. What does Jesus' fast in the wilderness teach about Holy Spirit and fasting?

d. When did Jesus tell disciples to use fasting as a breakthrough tool for hard things?

DISCUSSION: Why does Jairus' story resonate with nearly everyone? Can you relate a time when you were in similar circumstances?

Chapter Seven

Blocks to Healing

ONE NIGHT AT AN OHIO HOME CHURCH, A LADY ASKED FOR prayer for an impossible situation. As the result of an accident, her jaw was deteriorating; she'd grown fearful about her doctor's report. As we prayed, we took authority over fear and commanded a creative miracle to take place. Later that night, we knew a miracle had happened when she tearfully told us her pain and fear about her prognosis were gone. However, her testimony got even better. The next week, she went to her doctor. Her jaw had shifted into its correct position, deterioration was reversed, and bone density had returned to normal. Understanding authority makes things happen in the heavenlies.

Each week our prayer list from around the world grows longer with more healing needs. Sunday morning services see great response to words of knowledge and general calls to come forward for physical, spiritual, and other requests. Many seekers are supernaturally healed, but sometimes healing doesn't happen. A multitude of reasons may account for why some receive while others go away empty-handed. Basically, those ailing or praying don't understand why healing occurs or doesn't. You can be cognizant of your rights and authority in the Lord, but you also need to recognize your responsibilities. If you're seeking a healing that doesn't happen, maybe you should assess what's blocking that healing.

What Did Jesus Do?

Jesus had been in the land of Genessaret, and many miracles had occurred as well as a confrontation with Jewish scribes and Pharisees (see Matt. 15:21-28; Mark 7:24-30). He left for Tyre and Sidon. Not wanting people to know He was there, He entered a house secretively (see Mark 7:24). His attempts to get alone, however, didn't work. A Greek woman, a Syro-Phoenician, came in, fell at His feet (in Mark), and asked Him to cast a demon from her young (in Mark) daughter who was "severely demon possessed" (Matt. 15:22). Unlike other times when people asked Him to heal or deliver them, Jesus didn't respond. She continued to ask, though (see Mark 7:26). He still ignored her, and disciples urged Him to send her away. This woman wasn't deterred.

Mark says He finally acknowledged her. Before He answered, though, He said He was sent to lost Jews, not Gentiles (see Matt. 15:24). She again wasn't discouraged. However, when her pleas didn't get action, in desperation, she worshiped Him and said, "Lord, help me" (Matt. 15:25). His next words were negative, not acquiescing to a healing. He wouldn't agree to heal her daughter because that would take the children's bread and throw it to "little dogs" (Matt. 15:26). She answered that although what He said was true, dogs lying beneath the table could get crumbs that fell on the floor. That response touched Jesus. He expressed that her great faith had made her daughter whole. She *was* delivered that very hour (see Matt. 15:28). When the woman arrived home, her daughter was healed and lying in bed (see Mark 7:30).

Healing of the Gentiles

This story describes a major block to healing. Though Jesus often responded to desperation to heal and deliver, this time was different. Usually, He was willing; but for this one, He ignored the woman then gave her a reason for not healing her daughter. She was a Gentile and thus considered a dog. He'd referred to lowly animals earlier when teaching not to give treasures to "dogs" or to "cast your pearls before swine" (Matt. 7:6), a Jewish allusion to Gentiles. She was a Greek, and healing wasn't promised to sinners. Can you imagine your reaction if Jesus had called you a dog? Most would've given up or become insulted. Though she understood His analogy, she didn't grow discouraged or respond negatively. Despite His reaction and words, she was still convinced of and focused on the Master's abilities. She had a one-track mind, set on deliverance.

That connection between sin and sickness has been debated often and discussed in Chapter Two, "The Finished Work." This story also exemplifies that concept. When you become saved, you receive salvation and healing. However, when you don't accept Him as Lord, He's not obligated to heal you. The psalmist said, "If I regard iniquity in my heart, the Lord will not hear" (Ps. 66:18). In the New Testament, the blind man whom Jesus healed said, "God does not hear sinners" (John 9:31). Salvation and healing go hand in hand, so without salvation a piece is missing. I once read that "Asking for healing while refusing to be led by the Spirit [in salvation] is like asking a carpenter to repair the house while refusing to let him into the house."[1] Sadly, many want healing but not the Healer. However, that doesn't mean unbelievers can never be healed.

Naaman is an example of a Syrian rather than a Jew being healed after he obeyed the prophet's word (see 2 Kings 5:9-14). The Roman centurion's servant was healed by Jesus (see Luke 7:1-10). This healing of the Greek woman's daughter also shows the unsaved can be healed. However, principles should be observed for that to occur. First, believe; then keep asking. Persistence breaks through that healing barrier, while giving up negates the blessing. Walls of sickness fall when you persevere. If you ask Him multiple times like this lady, He doesn't forsake those who seek Him (see Ps. 9:10). Also, her reaction to His negative comments and His ignoring her speaks to me. She responded in humility, not entitlement or over-sensitivity when Jesus ignored her pleas or compared her to dogs. Emotional reactions aren't what get His attention. Faith and perseverance touch the Lord, no matter who you are.

The Children's Bread

Jesus' alluding to the children's bread as a healing block had meaning to the woman. Bread was considered sustenance, crucial and basic to life in ancient Israel and other cultures. It's mentioned often for supernatural provision. Elijah was kept alive by meat and bread from ravens while Obadiah assured 100 prophets' lives by hiding them in caves and feeding them bread (see 1 Kings 17:6; 18:4). When Jesus taught disciples to pray, He said to ask God to give "daily bread" (Matt. 6:11). The enemy tempted Jesus with bread in the wilderness, and He's the Bread of life (see Matt. 4:3; John 6:35). Like bread, healing is crucial to the body. Jesus said, "It is not good to take the children's bread and throw it to the little dogs" (Matt. 15:26), but this woman countered by saying she'd settle for crumbs the dogs eat that fall from their master's table. That use of *master* tells me she understood who was in control. The Greek word for *crumbs* is *psichion*, "a little bit or morsel."[2] She had such faith in the Master that she realized a morsel of healing from Jesus would be sufficient to deliver her daughter. A crumb from the Master brings great things.

I love His calling healing "the children's bread" because other references to bread and children exist. Jesus explained that if a son asks his earthly father for bread, a fish, or an egg, even flawed human fathers won't give that son a stone, serpent, or scorpion (see Luke 11:11-12). You love your children enough to provide their needs and desires; so you give good things, not bad. Knowing that, "If you then, being evil, know how to give good gifts to your children, how much more will your Father who is in heaven give good things to those who ask Him!" (Matt. 7:11). God is kinder and greater than human parents, so you can expect good things when you ask for bread, your healing. Luke quotes Jesus' words and specifies one of those good things—Holy Spirit (see Luke 11:13). Jesus came to earth to teach, heal, and deliver in Holy Spirit's power. Through Holy Spirit, you're assured of healing, not sickness, because that would be a stone instead of bread. Healing is God's children's bread, and His will is to heal them. He won't give you anything else but that healing. Not a stone or serpent or scorpion.

Fear

Fear is an enormous block that impedes healing because it ties God's hands. This Gentile woman believed in her being that Jesus was the Answer to her daughter's needs, so she persisted until He healed her. She demonstrated an important principle: Great faith rather than fear touches Jesus (see Matt. 15:28). She wasn't a Jew, but she knew He was the Lord. She called out like Bartimaeus did—"Have mercy on me, O Lord, Son of David" (Matt. 15:22). At times, have you felt He was ignoring your pleas? When you think He isn't listening, you may grow angry, fearful, or discouraged. However, many of Jesus' stories show that faith and determination are linked together. What if this lady had given up instead of persisting or had operated in fear instead of faith?

In a different deliverance, Jesus addressed how fear makes you ineffective in healing. After the Transfiguration, He came down from the mountain, and a great multitude with healing needs awaited Him, including a difficult deliverance (see Matt. 17:14-21). One man approached with his epileptic, mute son. A demon caused intense manifestations, including bruising when it left him. The boy's dad told Jesus that disciples had tried but couldn't cast it out, so He told them the necessity of preparation. Another issue He mentioned was their "unbelief," or fear that something is too big for God (Matt. 17:20). I understand their inability to exorcise the demon that displayed so powerfully. That could impact even the most spiritual. However, looking at symptoms, allowing fear to creep in, or being dumbfounded by manifestations are significant blocks to receiving or facilitating healing and deliverance. They're all parts of fear. After Jesus rebuked disciples for not healing the boy, they brought him to Jesus, the spirit became evident, and He cast it out.

Many who seek healing come with gentler words that still speak fear: "I'm afraid, scared, stressed, concerned, upset...." Fear sounds better when you call it *worry*, but our former pastor used to say, "Worry is fear, and fear is sin" (see Rom. 14:23). Jesus said not to worry about necessities in your life—food, clothing, drinks—because your worry accomplishes nothing (see Matt. 6:27). As you minister to others or believe for your own healing, "God has not given [you] a spirit of fear, but of power and of love and of a sound mind" (2 Tim. 1:7). As Peter strolled across the water toward Jesus, he proceeded fine while he looked at the Lord and not at the wind and waves (see Matt. 14:29-30). When he took his eyes off Jesus and focused on the situation's difficulty, fear slapped him in the face, and he sank. During a storm, Jesus asked disciples, "Why are you fearful, O you of little faith?" He then rebuked the storm, not those who came to Him for an answer (Matt. 8:26). As you come, He welcomes your seeking Him then rebukes your life's storms. However, approaching Him shouldn't be because of fear. Whether you face powerful demons or boisterous waves, fear can't be part of an overcoming scenario. Paul says not to be anxious about anything but to give requests to God who gives peace (see Phil. 4:6-7). Fear is a crippler and negates God's plan.

Doubt and Unbelief

Doubt and unbelief are byproducts of fear and a deterrent to receiving or being used in healing. Unbelief blocks faith and consequently healing. Paul mentions "an evil heart of unbelief" (see Heb. 3:12). "Evil" is a strong word to describe something that many Christians exhibit regularly. He later identifies unbelief as the reason the children in the wilderness couldn't enter the Promised Land (see Heb. 3:19). Unbelief hinders your entering your own promised land of healing. Before Jesus delivered the possessed young man, his father voiced his belief but also for Jesus to help his unbelief. That's a wonderful thing to ask the Lord. Jeremiah reminds you nothing is too hard for God (see Jer. 32:17), but unbelief ties His hands.

That's happened many times as people asked me for prayer. However, their words of unbelief and skeptical looks said doubt would impede healing. If you don't guard against it, doubt tiptoes in and seeds are planted into your spirit—internet articles, symptoms, a doctor's report, well-intended words. That's why asking Jesus to help your unbelief is important if your faith feels shaky. Once the boy's dad got beyond the doubt, Jesus could do His work. As He healed the young man, He rebuked the unclean spirit and commanded it to come out. The spirit cried out, sent him into convulsions, exited, and left him as dead. As Jesus took his hand and lifted him, the boy arose. Then Jesus gave him back to his dad (see Mark 9:25-27; Luke 9:42). Doesn't that paint a picture of you with your heavenly Father? Jesus heals you and lays you in the Father's arms of love and protection. The tighter you hold on to Him, the tighter He holds on to you.

When Jesus taught about mountain-moving faith, the first part of His instructions were to, "Have faith in God" (Mark 11:22). What a simple, yet profound statement! He follows it by saying if a person speaks, doesn't doubt in his heart, but believes, he'll have his answer (see Mark 11:23). After they saw the withered fig tree, Jesus taught disciples that whatever they "ask[ed] in prayer, believing," they'd receive if they didn't doubt in their hearts (Matt. 21:21-22). The word He used for *doubt* is *diakrino*, "which connotes a conflict with oneself, in the sense of hesitating...wavering between hope and fear."[3] Instead of speaking to mountains to be gone, you erect mountains by fear and doubt coming from your heart through your mouth. I like that He mentions the heart as the place you should purge doubt. Your heart is the core of your being; if you want to be healed, doubt has no place there. Faith is in your spirit man, not your logical man. Despite what logic says, you should listen to faith and not let doubt drive results. Conflicts occur as fear and doubt sneak in, but doubt can't be present for healing to take place. Asking petitions of God with doubt in your heart makes you unstable (see James 1:6). F.F. Bosworth says: "If the farmer, without any definite promise, can have faith in nature, why can't the Christian have faith in the God of nature."[4] I want to add something—have faith in the nature of God. When you do, doubt can't be there.

All Things

Another block to healing is placing limits on God. In Matthew's version of the boy's deliverance, Jesus told disciples that if their faith were as a grain of mustard seed, the impossible would happen. Then, in Mark He reiterated to the distraught father that, "If you can believe, all things are possible" (Mark 9:23). Belief is having faith for *all things*; unbelief limits that. In Jesus' statement, *believe* is *pisteuo*, "to trust in, have faith in, be fully convinced of, acknowledge, rely on."[5] Being fully convinced of His ability allows you to know that *all things* include no exceptions for big needs. Jesus gave a qualification for receiving—you must believe healing will happen. Belief is total *pisteuo* on Jesus' ability and that when He says "all things are possible," nothing is excluded. That includes whatever seems far too massive to repair—a body riddled with cancer, a womb that can't conceive, a son so badly possessed demons throw him in the fire. John says you don't receive just a limited amount of/from Him. Because of Holy Spirit, you can get all you want of God (see John 3:34). You settle for too little when *all things* are accessible.

One Sunday morning after I had a word of knowledge, a mother stood in the prayer line for her daughter. She told those of us on the altar team about her daughter's problems then asked us to pray that doctors would discover what was wrong. That request is typical of doubt about the Lord's *all things* capabilities. I told her to set her sights higher on what Jesus Himself could do for her—the *all things* to which she's entitled. Many settle for less than they have available as King's children. Though Jesus often uses a surgeon's hand in healing, the surgeon isn't the healer, just an educated man. Jesus created you then paid for your healing, even for what doctors can't diagnose. Can you wrap your mind around that promise? *All things!*

Ready and Able

Another block to healing is not being prepared. As David was going to kill Goliath, King Saul offered his armor, but David refused because he hadn't tested it (see 1 Sam. 17:39). Instead, he used rocks and a slingshot that had served him well in the past, so he was equipped for victory over the giant. When you minister, if you haven't prepared, you arrive at your battle with no armor or with untested armor. Prayer, especially, makes you comfortable in the battle because God, not man, equips you. Jesus prepared often through prayer, so He was ministry-ready. His secluded time readied Him for healing needs. Once, for example, He rose before daylight and went to a solitary place to pray when Peter and others came looking for Him to tell Him some were seeking Him (see Mark 1:35-39). After Jesus healed the man's possessed son, He told how lack of preparation can block healing. Disciples asked why they couldn't cast the demon out, and Jesus explained that, "This kind can come out by nothing but prayer and fasting" (Mark 9:29). Those who operate in gifts of healing and miracles must show up ready and able to effect healing and deliverance. If you know you'll be going to a service where you may be called upon to pray for others, you should arrive ready.

Jesus' inner circle learned about preparation in Gethsemane (see Matt. 26:36-46). Although He'd already told them what was to come, they didn't have the full picture. He left to pray regarding His rapidly approaching ordeal. Three times He returned; disciples were sleeping and not praying, despite His telling them twice (see Luke 22:40, 46) to "Pray that you may not enter into temptation" (Luke 22:40). That admonition became reality. As a result of their lack of prayer, when events of the next few hours unfolded, they weren't ready for what happened and thus entered into the temptation of which He'd spoken. The "disciples forsook Him and fled" while Peter denied Him (see Matt. 26:56, 70). Had they been prayer-ready, choices would have likely been different.

Being prayer-ready when I know I'm going to minister has served me well over the years, but sometimes the prayer need isn't planned. One afternoon as I went into our local Walmart, an elderly minister was leaving, looking pale and thin. He told me he was suffering from a serious condition. When I said I'd pray, he settled on the end shelf of an empty checkout counter at the store's entrance. His pain showed in his expression as he looked into my face. Many with disapproving glances walked by faster; but I still prayed with my hand on his head, gray from many years of prayer for others. As I finished, he stood up, moved around, stretched, laughed, and declared the pain was gone. That unplanned encounter touched that man who'd given a great portion of his life into God's ministry. As an added bonus, not everyone scurried by. While he and I were still talking, two others asked for prayer. That wasn't a time I'd anticipated needing to be prayer-ready, but how grateful I was that I had gone prayed-up.

These "coincidences" are wonderful times for God to show His power and might. After the Shunammite woman's son came back to life, a few chapters later, another story about her describes divine timings. Elisha prophesied that the land would experience seven years of famine and said she should leave. She obediently went to the land of the Philistines. After seven years she returned to find her house and lands taken. She approached the king to plead for restoration. Elisha's servant "just happened" to be with the king that day and was telling him about Elisha's miracles. As he was sharing about her son's resurrection, the Shunammite woman came in (see 2 Kings 8:1-6). Because of this godly timing, her property was restored. God's chance encounters are powerful intersections to accomplish much.

As often happened with Jesus, you may be going about the business of life when you're called upon to pray for others' dire needs—at your seat in church, your child's T-ball game, the entrance to Walmart. Often it comes at the most inconvenient moments when you've run to the grocery without make-up or in your tennis shoes, green from mowing the lawn. In Acts, Peter was also going about life's business. He may have had a big day planned to catch up on his ministry duties, spend time with his family, or maybe just rest. The Lord changed those plans, though, when men came to him "imploring him not to delay in coming to them" (Acts 9:38). This was a day when Peter didn't have time to go into his prayer closet for intense prayer. If he'd known in advance, he could have prepared spiritually, but often you must act upon the need immediately. Peter had to be ministry-ready for this dire need: Tabitha had died and needed to be raised. He responded. The result was a resurrection.

Jesus' power was amazing on earth, but He left us with our own healing mandate. Like Jesus expected the fig tree to be producing though it wasn't the season for figs (see Mark 11:13), you should be constantly producing the fruit of healing. Jesus taught that He'd take away branches that don't bear fruit (see John 15:2), and Paul says to be "ready in season and out of season" (2 Tim. 4:2). In other words, show up, prayed-up, because prayer needs are often spontaneous. Being ready *in and out of season* is a 24-7-365 job because people and their needs matter so much to the Lord and, as His hands on earth, to you, too. The healing of the demon-possessed son occurred as Jesus and His inner circle were descending from the mountain after the most intense glory event recorded in Scripture. A deliverance wasn't Jesus' objective that day. At the bottom, they encountered many with healing needs, including this possessed boy. Had they known in advance, they could've prepared; but this father approached them desperately, unexpectedly. Jesus' telling disciples what was needed for victory shows you should make prayer and fasting your lifestyle. Your next intersection may be with someone whose existence or freedom depends on you.

Judging

Another block to healing is negatively judging God's choice of whom He wants to use or how He wants to heal. One day, Jesus had been teaching multitudes so hungry for the Word they stood on the shore while He taught from a boat (see Matt. 13:1-2). After He sent them away, He returned to Nazareth, where He was reared. There, He also taught in synagogues, but those in Nazareth responded differently from other places. Elsewhere throngs had surrounded Him, voraciously grasping every word and miracle. In contrast, in Nazareth they were shocked, suspicious, and offended about how He could have such wisdom and mighty works (see Matt. 13:54, 57). They were His own people and should've realized His substance, character, and calling. Instead, they were side-tracked by being too familiar with Him. They knew his parents—Joseph, the carpenter, was His father; Mary was His mother. They could recite His brothers' names and still lived around His sisters (see John 6:42; Matt. 13:55-56). Instead of accepting and worshiping Him in

His deity, they "were offended at Him" (Matt. 13:57) and judged Him to be no one special.

Suspicion, envy, and self-seeking are aspects of judging and bring confusion and evil (see James 3:16), while impacting receiving. The misjudging in Jesus' hometown hindered their healing because "He did not do many mighty works there because of their unbelief" (Matt. 13:58). Mark says Jesus "*could do* no mighty works" (Mark 6:5-6). Nazareth citizens probably needed those miracles as critically as anywhere, but they missed that opportunity. Their judging and unbelief tied Jesus' hands from accomplishing what they greatly needed. He said, "A prophet is not without honor except in his own country and in his own house" (Matt. 13:57). Does that scenario sound familiar?

As you move into God-ordained ministries, you're received and celebrated wherever you go. In your families, churches, or hometowns, though, you're often denigrated because people remember you. They babysat for you or saw you sweating at the gym. They can enumerate your prior bad choices. Paul understood these types of trials because others were suspicious of him throughout his ministry because of his former character and choices (see Acts 9:26). After some see what God's accomplishing through you, they don't think of you as God's anointed vessel but as someone with familiarity and a past. I've also heard envy from some, even those closest who believe they'd be a better choice for your ministry. The truth is they're not called to that role, anointed, or couldn't/wouldn't do the necessary work.

You miss much because you judge God's message by the messenger. I've seen many instances of God healing through unlikely people, even children. A while back I saw a lady for the first time in years. She told me that when we were teenagers, we were at a church dinner, and I received a word of knowledge about her. She'd been experiencing abdominal issues where I'd indicated. As I laid my hands on her, she was healed and hasn't had that issue now for nearly fifty years. God chooses whom He uses, and you may not understand His choices because you don't comprehend others' value like God does (see 1 Sam. 16:7). The Lord rarely chooses the best in the world's eyes but always employs those with His anointed touch. Today, many preachers are elevated in the world's eyes, but answers often come not from the king but a shepherd boy who slays the giant or from a Carpenter with callused hands and a dusty robe. Or maybe it comes through you.

Sometimes you wrongly judge yourself by thinking you're not good enough to come to Jesus. Many variables keep people from approaching—preconceived biases, a feeling of worthlessness, others' opinions. But then, like the lady with the issue of blood, desperation drives them toward that humble Master. What a lesson! God doesn't arbitrarily choose whom He'll use or whom He'll heal. Those who go to Jesus get His touch. He proved often He didn't prefer those the establishment did—tax collectors, sinners, lowly fishermen, lepers. He loves all equally (see Acts 10:34), and His criteria is different from the world's. What a promise that He will perfect that which concerns you (see Ps. 138:8), and that includes healing.

Words

I've written much about the power of words as a healing help or block. Words can impede your healing when they speak fear and doubt. Any time you voice negativity, you speak that reality into being and negate God's plan. Jesus taught about speaking fear when He said don't worry, *saying* what will you eat, drink, or wear (see Matt. 6:31). The fact that He said not to speak your worries says that voicing those fears creates dynamics that impede God. When an angel spoke to Zacharias that Elizabeth would bear a son (see Luke 1:13), he doubted. The angel smote him mute until after the baby was born. Why? God had a plan for John the Baptist to come into the world to prepare the way for His Son. However, doubt spoken by Zacharias or others may have aborted that plan. Rather than his communicating damaging words, Zacharias became mute. You should be careful with your own words and with whom you share secrets because their words are powerful, too. Words, even those said about you, can derail God's planned miracle. Others' words about your situation make a great difference, especially as curses to afflict you.

As the Shunammite woman sought the prophet to raise her dead son, she didn't speak about the death to her husband, Elisha's servant, or to Elisha but said, "It is well" (2 Kings 4:26). Her promised son lay dead, but she never let that pass from her lips because she knew God's word held more authority than even death. Facts you see versus what you've been promised may be different, so you should guard your mouth and speak only God's reality. Elisha returned, and the boy was raised from the dead (see 2 Kings 4:30-35). What you expect to happen is reflected by your words, so your mouth should speak His promises or not speak at all. Solomon said, "A fool's mouth is his destruction, and his lips are the snare of his soul" (Prov. 18:7). He also said, "The words of the wise... and...of scholars are like well-driven nails" (Eccles. 12:11). You should use words like nails to ensure your healing rather than to secure your coffin. With words you create the reality in which you walk.

Despite Jesus' initial reaction, the Greek woman didn't allow herself to fall into the negativity trap. Instead of destructive words, her response was, "Yes, Lord" (Matt. 15:27). How that word, *yes*, can change your destiny as you agree with Jesus' words. Instead of fighting against what He's said, agreeing with Him brings change. It speaks of faith in His wisdom. After she said that, the woman humbled herself and worshiped, then said, "Lord, help me" (Matt. 15:25). When nothing else gets through to the Master, words of worship touch Him. Too often you focus on what He can do for you rather than the wonder of who He is. He loves your adoration; if He seems far away, worship catches His attention. It's the great equalizer that lifts you above the natural and into the spiritual realm. It lifts even Gentiles to a place of honor and brings healing.

Other Blocks

Not only can these impediments block your healing, but many other hindrances should be eliminated. God's heart is love, so He can't abide behaviors that don't align with His character. Love makes you want good, not bad things for others. Peter instructs you not just to love but to love "fervently [and] with a pure heart" (1 Pet. 1:22). If you love people intensely and your heart is pure, you prefer others. Even the unlovable. Seeing others from love's perspective is easier when you realize God loves everyone as much as He loves you, even those who are unkind. Anything that violates His law of love impedes your healing and moving into your God-ordained destiny (see Isa. 59:2). As I've said before, love is important in healing, more than asserting your faith and hope (see 1 Cor. 13:13).

God can't look past your sin when you come with petitions. Things God despises must go on that list:

> *These six things the Lord hates, yes, seven are an abomination to Him: a proud look, a lying tongue, hands that shed innocent blood, a heart that devises wicked plans, feet that are swift in running to evil, a false witness who speaks lies, and one who sows discord among brethren* (Proverbs 6:16-19).

This powerful passage describes how many Christians operate daily. Pride and arrogance are about "me" and demonstrate a self-focused nature rather than one centered on Him and others. Those people often work for the Lord from a motive of self-promotion and acknowledgment. When you minister for the good of others, you don't focus on your own issues but on how He can use you. Changing from the self mode transforms you and makes you more pleasing to the Father. James says, "Selfish ambition [brings] disorder and every evil practice" (see James 3:16 NIV). *Evil* is a strong word to be used about the actions of many Christians. Obviously, *self* can't be your focus if you want a healing ministry.

Other traits mentioned in the passage speak of integrity issues, which show what's in your heart. Lying, murder, purposely doing evil, concocting wicked plans, and stirring up trouble show a spiteful character. Other behaviors may seem innocent, but they can stand between you and God. Some you should eliminate are "malice...deceit, hypocrisy, envy" (1 Pet. 2:1), "bitterness, wrath, anger, clamor...evil speaking" (Eph. 4:31). These are from that *self*-motivation stance. Paul calls these and similar character traits "works of the flesh" (Gal. 5:19), which can rise up in any of us. God hates many other flesh works, like a "perverse mouth" (see Prov. 8:13). We should please God, and we can't do that by operating in the flesh (see Rom. 8:8).

Other personal characteristics impact healing. Some never learn the importance of submission to leadership (see Neh. 9:17), from teachers to parents to policemen to pastors. Disobedience is another block. Both lack of submission and disobedience are aspects of rebellion and linked to witchcraft. Though King Saul perceived that his reasons were good, disobedience caused him to lose the kingdom. During his speech to Saul, Samuel defined stubbornness "as iniquity or idolatry" (1 Sam. 15:22-23). Though you may see these behaviors as just part of your personality, God wants them gone. Paul says, "If we live in the Spirit, let us also walk in the Spirit," eliminating works of the flesh like envy or conceit that impact our spiritual walk (Gal. 5:25-26). Dwelling in Holy Spirit allows flesh to take a back seat. Do any of these undesirable attributes, which God hates, reside in you? If you check your heart daily to find if these or other sins exist, you can repent then walk according to Holy Spirit. All of us have human traits with which we contend, and some aren't pretty. My mother used to say, "I don't want those ugly things in this house," as she pointed to herself. Through repentance each block to healing and to your destiny can be eliminated and free the way for the Healer. Then, watch heaven's doors open!

Conclusion

One night as I prayed, I saw a vision of my sister Becky beside a Japanese symbol, which I later found out represented long life and prosperity. She told me doctors had found a lump in her breast, likely malignant because of the mass' size. She'd told only a few people because she was aware of words' importance and didn't want lack of faith spoken. God gave her a promise through my vision—she'd have long life and prosperity. We held on to that promise and didn't fall into unbelief. During surgery, the lump was massive as doctors first cut; then it disappeared. Protecting her words saved her life through that miracle. What you and others speak is important in receiving your healing and keeping it.

God's given not only healing but *all things* as a perk for His children. Healing is essential, like bread for the children, and God doesn't withhold good things. As a Christian, healing is your inheritance, part of those *all things*, both for you and through you for others. Helping others to be saved and healed gets your eyes off your own problems. With the gifts comes responsibility. That's part of the instruction He gave, so you should be ready when needs arise. Though you know healing is yours as a Christian, many things can block it. Hindrances like sin, fear, and unbelief impede healing; but repentance, faith, and perseverance can make it happen. Asserting faith and stepping out of the fear camp opens the door for your own and others' healings. If you assess yourself daily, God can reveal what's not pleasing to Him. Removing what hinders healing opens the way for Him to bless through you or other unexpected sources.

Questions to Ponder

Answers in the Appendix

1   a.   How was Jesus' response to the Syro-Phoenician woman different from His other healings?

      b.   Tell the meanings of Psalm 66:18 and James 9:31 in regard to healing.

      c.   Give examples of exceptions to this.

      d.   What principles must be observed for this to happen?

2   a.   Give biblical examples of when bread's importance was demonstrated.

      b.   Describe the conversation between Jesus and this woman about the children's bread.

      c.   Explain how the Bible deals with the children's bread.

3   a.   Fill in the blanks: "Great ___ rather than ___ touches ___."

      b.   Why might fear have been a reason disciples couldn't cast out the demon from the boy?

      c.   Jesus didn't rebuke the disciples about not speaking to the storm but about what?

4   a.   How does the father of the demon-possessed son show how to deal with unbelief?

      b.   Jesus' laying the boy in his dad's arms represents what about relationship with the Father?

      c.   Where do you need to purge doubt?

5   a.   What did Jesus promise you can have?

      b.   What must you do to receive these things? Can you share a time when God gave you something big you'd asked for?

6   a.   What prepares you for great deliverances?

       b.   How did lack of prayer in Gethsemane negatively impact disciples?

       c.   Why should you stay prayer-ready?

       d.   Give one Bible story about God's unexpected timing.

       e.   How should you be like the fig tree?

7   a.   How was Jesus judged wrongly in His hometown?

       b.   What happened there as a result?

       c.   What did Jesus mean in Matthew 13:57?

       d.   How does misjudging yourself impact going to Jesus?

8   a.   How can your or others' words about you affect your promises from God?

       b.   What does Solomon say about words?

       c.   How did the Greek woman speak words that brought about healing?

9   a.   List things God hates.

       b.   Give other character traits that could block your healing.

       c.   What did Samuel compare to disobedience?

DISCUSSION: Which principle from the story of the Syro-Phoenician woman or the man with the possessed son speaks most to you?

Chapter Eight

Compassion

WADE AND I USED TO PASTOR A SMALL CHURCH WHERE WE ALL felt like family; so parishioners' extended families mattered, too. That's why when one member came with a report about her daughter-in-law, compassion welled inside us. She and her husband were desperate after trying many years to become pregnant, even going through rounds of unsuccessful fertility treatments. We not only prayed that morning but continued to keep her in our hearts. Soon, the report came—she was pregnant. However, excitement was subdued a couple months later when the mother-in-law came for another prayer for her unborn grandchild. Doctors said the mother must stay on bedrest, and chances were good the baby would have Down Syndrome. Instead of being devastated at this news, we responded with compassion and again took that mother and baby to the Lord. By the next week, she was back at work, and tests showed the baby was fine. We continued to intercede for both during the coming months; she delivered a beautiful, perfect, full-term, eight-pound girl. Our compassion reached the Lord's heart of compassion.

We live in a *me* world where parents sacrifice families for their own fulfillment. Where addicts destroy theirs and others' lives for the pleasure of a high. Where employees steal from employers because they feel they're owed more than a salary. Where even Christians ignore those in need if it doesn't suit their agendas. In essence, the *me* mindset has led us to forget an important Jesus trait—compassion. Some may feel pity or acknowledge another's plight but don't act with compassion because too much self exists—*my* house, *my* family, *my* needs, *my* money, *my* marriage, even *my* ministry. If you want to be used in the miraculous realm, you must embrace compassion. Jesus did.

What Did Jesus Do?

After Jesus' lengthy teaching on the mountain, He entered an unnamed city. A man "full of leprosy" (Luke 5:12) saw and approached Him; fell on his face in worship; and said if Jesus were willing, He could make him clean (see Matt. 8:1-4; Mark 1:40-45; Luke 5:12-16). As the leper bowed before Him, Jesus was "moved with compassion," put forth His hand, touched him, and said, "I am willing; be cleansed" (Mark 1:41). When He spoke, the leprosy left. Jesus charged him to tell no one but to go to the priest as a testimony, like God had instructed in Moses' time (see Lev. 13:1-3). However, the leper was so excited about his healing that he told many (see Mark 1:45). Word circulated about Jesus even more than previously, and throngs flocked to hear Him and be healed. As a result, He couldn't come openly into the city but stayed outside in less-populated areas. However, those in need still came to Him from "every direction" (Mark 1:45); so He withdrew to the wilderness to pray (see Luke 5:16).

Willing

Jesus often showed compassion by healing someone others considered unclean. This time, He felt compassion toward this man with an illness that ostracized him from society. By Jewish law, a leper was considered unclean and to be avoided. Obviously, Jesus knew the law and followed it by sending him to the priest. However, his violation of that law by touching the unclean man demonstrated His own law of love. He loved like you should—unconditionally. He didn't judge but stepped up to demonstrate willingness and compassion in action. With love as your law, you don't pick and choose upon whom you spend your compassion. Peter, who witnessed this miracle, later proclaimed that Jesus healed and delivered all "for God was with Him" (Acts 10:38). God's with you when you pray for healing, and He doesn't have favorites He blesses or ignores (see Rom. 2:11). Not everyone who comes to you is upstanding, clean, or even likeable, but you must treat each as Jesus did.

The leper said if Jesus were willing, he'd be healed. This sounds like many today who say they'll be healed if it's God's will. This story confirms that Jesus *is* willing to heal you. Before He touched the leper or the healing was manifested, the Lord wanted him to know for sure that He *was* "willing." The word *willing* is *thelo,* to "desire, will, take delight in. It carries the idea of being ready, preferring, and having in mind."[1] All those descriptions speak of Jesus. He desires, even delights in healing you. He prefers you, so He's ever ready because you're always on His mind. My husband says your picture is on the Lord's refrigerator. How could healing evade you when you're on His mind constantly? Because He loves and relishes helping you, you should go to Him with assurance. Too often, like the leper, you precede your request with *if* instead of coming to Him with certainty that healing *is* His will. Jesus' answer to this leprous man should negate your *if* mindset. The leper followed his *if* with a *can.*

As Jesus demonstrated in His prayer example (see Matt. 6:10), you're to ask for God's will in all you do. However, never did He pray about the Father's will for healing because God wants all to be healed. Romans 12:1 refers to God's willingness: "I beseech you therefore, brethren, by the mercies of God, that you present your bodies a living sacrifice, holy, acceptable to God." This multi-faceted scripture tells you to give your bodies as a sacrifice to Him. The Greek word for *bodies* is *soma*, "the body (as a sound whole)."[2] This carries great truth. For a sacrifice, Hebrews needed a sound, flawless animal, not one riddled with illness. God wants you to present yourself as a sacrifice to Him, but that means He wants your bodies "as a sound whole" so you can work for His Kingdom.

His compassion and willingness are part of His making your body whole. Getting past uncertainty about His will for healing allows you to say with "confidence...in Him, that if we ask anything according to His will, He hears us. And if we know that He hears us, whatever we ask, we know that we have the petitions that we have asked of Him" (1 John 5:14-15). You know His will is for you to live in divine health; so you can apply confidence that because He hears you, you're going to receive what you ask. Then, the next step is to receive healing as a result of faith. He wants to give more than you can imagine as you claim covenant rights by asserting faith and obtaining healing. He was/is willing to heal because "He delights in mercy" (Mic. 7:18). His compassion (mercy) changed a desperate man's life. He's still willing to heal you and change your desperate situations.

When your mind becomes renewed to understand His willingness, healing comes within reach (see Rom. 12:2). I love Old Testament stories that show God's heart of love for His people. One reference that speaks to me is after His people had sinned, He allowed them to be conquered by their enemies. Then, God raised judges to deliver them "for the Lord was moved to pity by their groaning" (Judg. 2:18). Another time though they'd sinned and deserved punishment, "His soul could no longer endure the misery of Israel" (Judg. 10:16). What a picture of God's character and depth of love for even His disobedient people! If His heart breaks by tribulations of people actively operating in sin, those walking in righteousness can be assured of His will for healing. As your groans and healing needs reach Him, His love makes Him attack and defeat your enemies, even the enemy of sickness. Healing *is* His will, or He would've ignored these lepers or the boy His chosen twelve couldn't heal. Healing is His will for you, too.

Moved with Compassion

Mark says that when the leper asked Jesus for healing, Jesus was "moved with compassion." He also demonstrated that concept when He saw sick multitudes and was "moved with compassion" (Matt. 14:14). Where love, power, and authority met was His compassion. Without reservation Jesus loved the unclean, undesirable, and hostile. Even during His arrest, He demonstrated compassion. When an angry Peter cut off the high priest's servant's ear, Jesus healed him (see Luke 22:51). Compassion doesn't judge or differentiate between people. John says you don't have God's love if you see your brother's need and "[shut] up [your] heart from him." The King James Version says when you shut up your "bowels of compassion" (1 John 3:17). The word *compassion* is *splachnizomai*, meaning "to be moved with deep compassion or pity."[3] The Greek for *bowels* is similar to the meaning of compassion—*splagchnon,* meaning "strengthened from...(the spleen); an intestine...pity or sympathy...inward affection, + tender mercy."[4] This speaks to me. The Greeks believed passionate and strong emotions originated in the bowels, or spleen.[5] How appropriate that the word *moved* is used with *compassion.* Just as your bowels demand to move and issue forth waste, so compassion should come forth as part of your nature to issue love, sympathy, affection, mercy, and healing.

Compassion comes from the core of your being as Holy Spirit moves on you. Those with great compassion and confidence in Him also have great healing anointing. If you have no compassion for the hurting, how can you bring healing? When Jesus went off by Himself, people ran to Him (see Mark 9:15). When the sick see where needs can be addressed, they follow expectantly. You should respond to them as Jesus did—with compassion. Because of His bowels of mercy, He didn't consider His sorrow or physical needs first. He just loved. Peter said, "All of you be of one mind, having compassion for one another; love as brothers, be tenderhearted, be courteous" (1 Pet. 3:8). Compassion gets beyond yourself. True compassion isn't self-centered but focused on others. You see through Jesus' eyes and feel their pain with His heart. Even when disciples healed on their own, they had confidence in His ability through them and compassion for the multitudes. We're now His disciples to take healing to the hurting.

His compassion showed in the miraculous provision of the 5,000 and 4,000 who were spiritually and physically hungry (see Matt. 14:20; 15:36). It showed in His calming waves for frightened disciples (see Mark 4:37-40). It showed with each healing that was personal both to the afflicted and to Him because the "Lord *is* merciful [compassionate] and gracious, slow to anger, and abounding in mercy" (Ps. 103:8). That compassion is your healing catalyst, too. Compassion for the sick is so important that as Jesus was teaching disciples about people being judged in the end time, He included that if you care for those in need, you also care for Christ (see Matt. 25:45). Through compassion, you want to help, and that opens healing's door.

Human Limitations

Compassion comes from the Father (see Rom. 9:15). That was part of Jesus' character and should be yours, too. His ministry was about people, and that meant His time wasn't His own because of His heart of compassion for hurts, afflictions, and pain. However, His human body also had limitations. As He trod those dusty roads with the sun scorching His olive skin, He grew hot, weary, hungry, thirsty. Once, he demonstrated His body's limitations while ministering by the sea. He had disciples keep a boat behind them in case they needed to escape the massive crowd pressing against Him and potentially crushing Him in their fervor for healing (see Mark 3:9). Another time when He knew that Pharisees were plotting His destruction, He left for His safety (see Matt. 12:14-15). His feeding the 4,000 was after He noted that the crowd could faint from hunger on their way home (see Matt. 15:32). He was aware of human limitations and the body's needs, so He reportedly stayed often in Bethany for rest, food, and fellowship (see Matt. 21:17). He often got alone to pray and be restored. Although my featured story about the leper doesn't directly say this, Jesus' staying in less-populated areas likely alludes to His human need for rest.

Human limitations are real. God intends for you to have balance and use wisdom, spiritually and physically. Frequently, though, compassion necessitates helping others despite your own needs. Though Jesus' physical limitations were important, His character of compassion considered others' needs before His own. Because of compassion for the multitudes, leaving was difficult when so many needed so much (see Matt. 9:36). Working for God should be a priority, but you should also be aware of your body's needs. In my childhood, multitudes drove many pain-filled miles in search of desperate healings. Great ministers like William Branham and A.A. Allen prayed hours for long lines of those ailing until the last person had felt God's touch through their hands. By that time, assistants often physically supported the preachers so they could finish and then be helped off stage. Their bodies paid a price as they were moved with compassion by massive numbers needing to be healed and delivered. Despite compassion for others, you also need to observe your human limitations.

Attacks

Compassion and human limitations are also tested by another source of stress—challenges of others, often Christian brothers and sisters. Once in the land of Genessaret, Jesus had not only performed many miracles but also had confrontations with Jewish religious leaders. Another time, as He taught in the synagogue, He saw a man with a withered right hand (see Matt. 12:9-14; Mark 3:1-6; Luke 6:6-11). As usual, scribes and Pharisees tried to entrap and accuse Him by seeing if He would heal on the Sabbath. He knew what they were thinking, but He still told the man to step forward. He asked temple leaders if it were lawful to do good and save a life on the Sabbath. He then asked them if a sheep had fallen into a pit on the Sabbath, would they get it out? He declared people to be of more value than sheep and noted with anger and grief the hardness of their hearts. He told the man to stretch out his hand. As he obeyed, it was healed (see Mark 3:4-5; Matt. 12:11-13).

This occurred on another Sabbath when Jesus entered a Pharisee leader's house to eat, and a man with dropsy was there. Again, lawyers and Pharisees watched to see what He'd do. Again, He asked who would refuse to rescue his livestock, this time a donkey or ox, out of a pit on the Sabbath. When they didn't answer, Jesus healed the man and let him go (see Luke 14:1-6). How sad that religion had devolved so they were more concerned about animals' needs than people's. Though Jesus condemned their traditions by His questions, the constant badgering surely took its toll. Being buffeted by others was part of Jesus' ministry and part of yours, too.

The enemy uses people's attacks to wear you down, impact your confidence, affect your sleep, and create a distraction. It erodes bodies and minds, so the enemy doesn't give up if he thinks he's found a weapon to defeat you. Because constant challenges, attacks, and persecution are exhausting, watching your associations is crucial. However, some of your most demanding relationships come not through attacks but rather from chronic takers. They deplete your energy when they repeatedly depend upon you to go to the Lord for their needs instead of finding relationship for themselves. God once told me to distance myself from those who continually drained me. When I learned to say no, some grew angry and went on the offensive against me. You should distinguish between those who are protégés and those who are parasites who exhaust you, leaving you depleted when your true godly assignment comes along.

At the land of Genessaret, many thronged Jesus for healing; but there, He was again challenged by contentious leaders. He stayed in someone's home and didn't want anyone to know, probably to rest because of the challenges and physical demands involved with healing (see Mark 7:24). After the leper spread the word about his healing, Jesus couldn't stay in the city but went to a deserted place. That didn't stop multitudes from pursuing Him for healing, though (see Mark 1:45). That tells me attacks are distractions because your calling is to help others, and your next assignment may be coming down the road. Dwelling on attacks keeps you from hearing the Lord and being ready when He calls. Like Jesus needed to get away to recharge, reflect, pray, and hear from God, time with your Father refocuses you and prepares your mind and body to hear His directions. If you don't observe your physical limitations, you'll have nothing to give others as you're about the Father's business.

His Sorrow

The passage about the leper wasn't exclusively when Jesus saw crowds and was moved with compassion, even sorrow. Once during his time in prison, John the Baptist had questioned Jesus' calling. How sad that must've made the Lord, yet He didn't send back an indignant response about John's unbelief. Jesus said to tell John of the miracles and healings—the blind, lame, leprous, deaf, dead, poor. Then John was killed. Jesus had recently been told about John's death and was impacted by the news, so He went alone by boat to a deserted location (see Matt. 11:4-5; 14:13). His reaction to John's death demonstrates His compassion and human sorrow.

He was omniscient and knew John's fate in advance; but they were cousins, just six months apart (see Luke 1:36). Though long before their births they were chosen to accomplish greatness, as boys, they probably had sleepovers at each other's houses or played tag on village streets. They'd likely been punished together as their godly parents molded their characters into extraordinary men. As teens, they may have worked on carpentry projects with Jesus' dad or hung out in the temple, learning about Scripture from John's father, a priest. There, they absorbed teachings they'd later repeat as hope to many. As men, they intimately knew each other's personalities and callings. How appropriate that John had been the one who baptized Jesus and heard God proclaim His Son's calling to the world (see Mark 1:9-11). They had relationship.

They'd both come to earth for "such a time as this" (Est. 4:14) when their presence would change history. Now, though, John had died horrifically at Herod's hands. Most likely, Jesus felt great sorrow about the man He so intimately knew and loved. He experienced human emotions and needed to get away, alone. He hurt, like you do. He loved, like you do. He had family, like you do. Relationships were important to Him, just as they are to you. His life-long buddy and cousin had suffered in prison and now was beheaded. It mattered to Him. Because He underwent and understood human emotions, "we do not have a High Priest who cannot sympathize with our weaknesses" (Heb. 4:14-15). He has compassion because He knows how you feel; He's experienced it all. This Savior delights in making the sick well because like John and the multitudes mattered to him, so do you. He gave beyond His fatigue, so His extreme sorrow at the loss of someone He loved didn't change His willingness to help the sick. After news of John's death and Jesus' going to be alone, His calling from God followed Him like those desperate crowds. The multitudes saw where He was going and ran ahead on foot to outdistance Him. Despite His own emotional needs, He tenderly and compassionately acted on His love rather than His own sorrow and healed them (see Matt. 14:13-14).

Desperation

The leper is an example of when Jesus healed the unclean because of compassion. Another story demonstrates Jesus' loving response to desperation. The day after healing the centurion's servant, He and many disciples went to a city called Nain. When He drew near the gate, a large crowd was gathered as a dead man, the only son of a widowed mother, was being carried out (see Luke 7:11-17). As the Lord saw the mother, compassion arose in Him; He told her, "Do not weep" (Luke 7:13). Although even being near a dead person was considered a defilement, He touched the open coffin and told the young man to arise (see Ezek. 44:25; Luke 7:14). The dead man sat up and started talking, and Jesus presented the son to his mom. This mother mattered because Jesus relates to a family's loss, just like with John's death. He's "near to those who have a broken heart" (Ps. 34:18). He was aware of this mother's pain and mourning and gave a resurrection. Isaiah prophesied that "In all their affliction, He was afflicted" (Isa. 63:9). Like a mother suffers for her child, He feels your pain. This particular scenario with a devastated mother probably resonated with Him because He was close to His own mother. He already knew what His fate would be and that His mother would mourn the loss of her precious Son. At the cross, He loved her so much He appointed John as her new son (see John 19:26). After this, He could die, "knowing that all things were now accomplished" (John 19:28), even taking care of His earthly relationships.

The Lord once used my love for my young daughter to demonstrate how a mother's love reaches the Master. One night I dreamed she was dying. As people milled around my house and looked at her lying there, no one took on that burden of compassion and prayed for her. When I awoke, the dream bothered me, even at church that morning. After worship, a lady requested prayer for her young grandson, diagnosed with cancer. Perched on my seat at the piano, I saw the congregation's reactions—just like those in my dream, shaking their heads and saying, "Isn't that terrible?" When the pastor led a formulaic prayer, compassion welled in me. As he finished, I asked to share my dream, emphasizing that my daughter represented that boy. I said we needed to pray again fervently and with compassion as if he were our own little boy because that day, he was. The assembly listened and took it to heart. We prayed, this time intensely and tearfully. I felt great peace. Later, his grandmother reported he was healed. He's long since graduated, served in the military, and now has a child of his own.

Conclusion

The definitions I read about *bowels* and *compassion* meant much to me as I wrote this book. As I said in my prologue, I grew sick a few weeks after beginning to research for this book. Doctors sent me for CT scans, which showed a significantly enlarged spleen. I was awaiting test results when I read that the definitions relate to the spleen. I cried. Even months later when doctors removed my spleen, I still knew even my spleen matters to Jesus, so I'm taking the limits off what He can do and am awaiting the new spleen He'll implant in me. If He cares enough to count the hair on my head (see Luke 12:7), He cares about everything concerning me— my kids, my job, my spleen. He spends His great compassion on us, no matter the request.

"The mercy of the Lord is from everlasting to everlasting...and His righteousness to children's children" (Ps. 103:17). Right now, you may think you're not worthy to come to Him. You may not be what the world considers clean, or you may think you come to Him way too often. He doesn't see worthiness like the world does or count the number of times you approach. Though you needed Him yesterday and the day before and the day before that, "His compassions fail not. They are new every morning" (Lam. 3:22-23). As you come each day, His brand-new compassion envelopes you for whatever you need, even a resurrection or a new spleen. Jesus understands human struggles and is willing to heal because He paid that price. As His representative you should be aware of your own needs but also get beyond yourself to love those desperate for the Master's touch through you.

Questions to Ponder

Answers in the Appendix

1   a.   How does Jesus' response to the leper's statement show his willingness to heal?

      b.   How does the Greek word for *willing* tell about Jesus' willingness to heal?

      c.   In Romans 12:1, how does the Greek word for *bodies* show God's will for healing?

      d.   What do examples from Judges 2:18 and 10:16 show about the Father?

2   a.   How do His healings show Jesus' compassion, even to the least?

      b.   Being "moved with compassion" refers to the bowels or spleen because Greeks believed what?

      c.   Fill in the blanks: "True ____ isn't ____-____ but ____ on others." Give an example of a time you've seen compassion in action.

3   a.   Give some of Jesus' human limitations.

      b.   What did He do to be ministry-ready but still observe His human needs?

      c.   Fill in the blanks: "God ____ for you to have ____ and use ____, ____ and ____.

4   a.   Who usually attacked Jesus?

      b.   How did He counter their criticism of His healing on the Sabbath?

      c.   How might others deplete you? Do you have a personal example?

5   a.   From this chapter, what made Jesus feel sorrow?

       b.   Why was Jesus close to John the Baptist? Give a scripture that says He feels emotions like you do.

6   a.   How did Jesus demonstrate His sensitivity to a mother's desperation in this chapter?

       b.   Give other biblical examples of God's responding to a parent's desperation.

       c.   When Jesus died, what was the last thing He accomplished?

DISCUSSION: How did the story of Jesus' compassion for both the leper and the dead son touch you?

Chapter Nine

Deliverance

My husband and I train others in deliverance, so we get frequent requests for help. Once, Wade was asked by a pastor to go to a home where a young man was demonstrating signs of demon possession. When Wade arrived, the man was unable to get out of bed by himself. His debilitating pain necessitated his taking frequent showers to ease that pain. He'd gotten so bad his family felt he was dying. Wade came in, discerned his spiritual needs, and ministered deliverance from an inherited familiar spirit that had attached itself through a generational curse. The man renounced the operation of that spirit and activities from his past that had been open doors for it to enter. Then Wade commanded the spirit to leave. Immediately, the young man's countenance changed. Before Wade left, he was up, moving, and asking for something to eat. The latest report is that he's no longer bedridden and doesn't need constant showers to mask pain. The demonic presence that left allowed the Lord to do a work in his body.

Warfare and deliverance are mentioned often in Jesus' ministry and should be part of your Christian walk. Warfare isn't won by your power here on earth but in the heavenly realm by His power. It's a spiritual battle, not one against people or other things you may consider as enemies. Your struggle for healing is against satanic powers because many sicknesses are actually demonic from which a person must be delivered in order to receive then keep his/her healing. You must be sensitive to and take authority over those spirits that come to wreak havoc.

What Did Jesus Do?

After Jesus calmed the waves, He and His disciples travelled to the other side of the sea to the country opposite of Galilee, the land of the Gadarenes/Gergesenes (see Matt. 8:28-34; Mark 5:1-20; Luke 8:26-39). After He left the boat, He had no time to rest because immediately a demon-possessed man (unclean spirit in Mark) came from the tombs and met Him (two men in Matthew). The man was living there and had been possessed a long time (see Luke 8:27), so demons were strong in violent ways. He was fierce, wouldn't let anyone pass by, and couldn't be tamed or bound. He'd often been strapped with shackles, chains, and irons on his feet but had pulled the chains apart and broken shackles into pieces. He wore no clothes. Spirits manifested by symptoms like seizures and cutting himself with rocks. He cried out day and night from the mountains and tombs (see Mark 5:5), and spirits often drove him into the wilderness.

When demons knew Jesus would command them to come from the man/men, they confronted Him and asked if He'd come to torment them before their time (see Matt. 8:29). Mark added that as the possessed man saw Jesus, he ran and worshiped Him. Jesus didn't argue with them but simply told the spirit to come out then asked its name (see Mark 5:6-8). The demons replied, "Legion," because many demons resided in him (see Mark 5:9). Those spirits knew they had to comply but asked Jesus if they could go into a group of 2,000 swine instead of out of the country or into the abyss (see Mark 5:10-13; Luke 8:31). Jesus allowed it, so they left the man and entered the swine. The entire passel of pigs ran violently down a cliff and drowned in the sea (lake in Luke). Swine keepers were appalled at the demonic warfare and perhaps their loss of livelihood, so they ran away and told others in the city what had happened. When the community went to confirm, they pled with Jesus to leave that region (in Mark). He got into the boat to leave, and the formerly possessed man begged to become a disciple and travel with Him. Jesus refused but told him to witness to others about what God had done. He did.

Demons' Operation

Many examples of Jesus' healings deal with demonic deliverance. Demons are constantly searching to oppress or possess bodies with the intention of destroying that person (see Mark 5:5). If they don't accomplish their purpose, they'll try again and are on the lookout for every opportunity. After the devil had unsuccessfully tempted Jesus on the mountain, he left "until an opportune time" (see Luke 4:13). The demons' pleas for Jesus to allow them to go into the swine showed their desire to inhabit bodies (even swine). Evil spirits are clever, crafty, and secretive so people won't perceive their existence. They're permitted to operate on earth for a limited period, which they demonstrated by telling Jesus not to make them leave before their time. Because of this, they attempt to maximize damage. Once they've gained access, that person/creature behaves differently, such as how the swine ran to get free. The changes when a demon enters a body can vary; the longer it stays, the more obvious and brazen it becomes. When demons manifest, the possessed person exhibits abnormal behaviors, from minor to life-threatening.

The demons that occupied this man in the tombs had obviously possessed him a long time because he was threatening and violent. He had supernatural strength to break his chains because demons are fierce and powerful. The possessed boy's father described similar manifestations— demons caused the son to foam at the mouth, wallow, gnash his teeth, fall to the ground, and become rigid. They also tried to kill him with fire and water (see Mark 9:20-22). The possessed man in the Capernaum synagogue cried in a loud voice and was thrown as the demon came out (see Luke 4:33, 35). I've witnessed many of these behaviors in possessed people. Their eyes often have unusual, disturbing stares; looks of hatred; seductive glances; or others. Demons also sometimes say inappropriate things like swearing or intimidating those ministering. As you deal with possession, be prepared for whatever may manifest, but don't let that shake your confidence.

Because they hide, you must judge in which spirit a person operates (see 1 Cor. 2:15). Just because he/she is seemingly okay, beware. Like the Syro-Phoenician woman worshiped Jesus, so did this man. However, she did so honestly and humbly while he was driven by demonic forces. I've seen people during a service who appeared to be worshiping legitimately, but something didn't ring true. This was apparent when the demon acted out and that person was later delivered from spirits. Demons are crafty, so use your gift of discernment about the spirit/Spirit in which others operate. Look to God for wisdom to know whom you should trust, for He's faithful to show you. Sometimes, demons emulate Holy Spirit to mask themselves, but you have the mind of Christ and Holy Spirit's revelation to perceive good and evil.

Many misconceptions exist about deliverance ministry. Some believe before you cast out demons, you must know their names because Jesus asked in this story. Though He did ask the name this time, it was after He ordered it to come out. Jesus' other deliverances show that knowing the demon's name is unnecessary. Although He often spoke to the type of evil spirit that was operating, He didn't call those spirits by a specific name in this or any other deliverance (see Mark 5, for example). He probably asked the name this time to show that during demonic warfare, you'll often deal with more than one spirit. Each time Jesus cast out demons, they obeyed because they had to bow to His commands. Spirits are also subject to you and me. Before beginning deliverance, you must know your conferred authority to cast them out (see Luke 10:20) and tell demons to leave, regardless of the type of evil spirit.

Demons and Sickness

The demonic is a major reason for health problems attributed to various factors. When someone gets sick, doctors consider explainable causes—viruses, bacteria, exhaustion, lifestyles, weakened immune systems, foods, family proclivities. Though psychologists and doctors blame behavioral or physical conditions on logical causes, this story says sometimes you should look beyond the medical field's understanding and into spiritual explanations. Some diagnoses can be valid, but this story gives another reason for illnesses—demons. Jesus' asking the demons' name showed they have various assignments that cause mental or physical conditions, and sometimes many may be inhabiting a person.

Many illnesses are listed as spirits, so consider the demonic as you pray for yourself and others. One ailment biblically connected to the demonic was when a man brought his son to Jesus with a "mute spirit" (see Mark 9:17). Later, as Jesus prayed, He called it a "deaf and dumb spirit" (see Mark 9:25). Another time, Jesus healed a demon-possessed, blind, and mute man (see Matt. 12:22). Though this story doesn't specifically say Jesus cast out demons of blindness and muteness, He healed possession, blindness, and muteness together. The implication is that possession caused all. The man in the tombs and the possessed son's symptoms are like many of today's sicknesses. For example, a demon was blamed for epilepsy and seizures when the son convulsed and was thrown (see Matt. 17:15). The King James Version uses the word *tare* instead of *convulse* (Mark 9:20 KJV), and that gives a more violent picture. That word, *sparasso*, indicates seizures and "to mangle...rend, tear."[1]

That intense definition gives a picture of the vicious damage a demon attempts to inflict. When the demon left after the son's seizure, it bruised him (see Luke 9:39), which could clarify unexplained bruises on many.

These stories and others also show demonic causes for emotional and psychological issues, labeled as mental illnesses. The Bible lists oppression as a condition that needed to be healed (see Acts 10:38). Behavioral problems such as violence and anti-social actions can be caused by demons. The demon-possessed man was destructive and cried out constantly and uncontrollably. He wandered erratically, stayed naked instead of clothed, and lived in caves (see Matt. 8:28; Mark 5:4-5; Luke 8:27, 29). The Treatment Advocacy Center estimates that about one third of the American homeless are seriously mentally ill.[2] This story names an alternate cause of homelessness as demons. Some labeled "mentally ill" actually need deliverance.

Cutting, like the demon-possessed man, is another destructive behavior afflicting especially the youth. That practice is attributed to self-loathing or unhealthy coping behaviors when this account blames demons (see Mark 5:5). Suicide and other destructive behaviors are also blamed on mental illness, but this account shows possession as its cause. After demons entered, swine ran down the hill to be drowned. Also, when the possessed son was thrown, people probably assumed he was trying to kill himself when demons were responsible (see Luke 9:33; Mark 9:22). I believe Judas committed suicide because of demonic possession (see Matt. 27:5; Luke 22:3). The suicide spirit is rife today, and you should take authority over it as a spirit. The term "mental illness" should more appropriately be called "demonic oppression or possession." However, though many evil spirits exist, don't become scared. Demons are subject to you in His name (see Luke 10:17).

Other Biblical References

The Bible demonstrates that demons have specific assignments to wreak havoc. Saul was God's choice for Israel's first king. His disobedience later resulted in his anointing being lifted and became an open door for possession by "a distressing spirit" (see 1 Sam. 16:14). When the Spirit of the Lord departs, a vacuum exists for evil spirits. Other kinds of spirits are mentioned in Scripture—lying (see 1 Kings 22:23), bondage (see Rom. 8:15), false (see Mic. 2:11), deceiving (see 1 Tim. 4:1) or seducing (in KJV), deaf and dumb (see Mark 9:25) or foul (in KJV), fear (see 2 Tim. 1:7), heaviness (see Isa. 61:3), sorrow (see 1 Sam. 1:15), error (see 1 John 4:6), antichrist (see 1 John 4:3), jealousy (see Num. 5:14), and ill will (Judg. 9:23). Another allusion is the spirit of infirmity, which describes different types of illnesses (see Luke 13:11). We've seen this spirit operate when seemingly unrelated ailments plague a person. They are dealt with by commanding the spirit of infirmity to cease its operation. Though evil and sickness exist in the demonic realm, the Bible also mentions good spirits like holiness (see Rom. 1:4), truth (see 1 John 4:6), and wisdom (see Deut. 34:9).

The sheer number of these spirits says many more exist and can possess humans. Spirits Jesus cast out were sometimes categorized as an "unclean spirit" (see Matt. 12:43). *Unclean* is *akathartos*, meaning "impure...foul."[3] Those words are general and could describe varied demons not mentioned in Scripture. Different biblical versions interpret Jesus' use of "unclean" as "defiling evil spirit" (MSG), "impure" (NIV), "evil" (EXB), and "demon" (TLB). No matter what their assignment, they're real and ready to inflict as much damage as possible. The good news is that you not only have authority, but you also can enlist help from heavenly angels. You aren't a victim to spirits but rather a victor over them through Jesus.

Recognizing Spirits

Because some afflictions are caused by demons, perceiving them in the Spirit is crucial. You can sensitize yourself to demonic operation through your Holy Spirit gift of discernment of spirits. Job's friend describes how he reacted to a demonic presence: "Fear came upon me, and trembling, which made all my bones shake. Then a spirit passed before my face; the hair on my body stood up" (Job 4:14-15). Many of you have probably experienced those sensations—you shake down to your bones as the hair on your arms stands up. Perceiving that demon's presence makes you better equipped for deliverance. As you become more experienced, you can recognize what kind of spirit to war against by the feeling or look associated with it.

When I was young, my mother had been a Spirit-filled Christian for several years, but she didn't fully understand spiritual warfare. Before I broke my arm the first time, she had a strange feeling, probably similar to the description in Job. She didn't connect that perception to a spirit that caused broken bones or calamities; so when she felt it again, she recognized it but didn't know to cover me in prayer. I broke my arm again—two more times in the next two years. The following year when she felt the spirit a fourth time, she understood about taking authority over the enemy. She had the church pray protection over me, but she didn't cover the rest of our family. That week, my brother broke *his* arm. Spirits are assigned for chaos and destruction. If you're aware of their presence, you can learn what they are, what they do, and how to get rid of them.

Open Doors

Anyone can be oppressed or possessed, even Christians, so how does it happen? While a Christian's spirit is intact, his/her mind and body may not be. Certain behaviors and practices allow satanic access into your mind and body. These are called open doors. Jesus referred to open doors when He said, "If therefore your eye is good, your whole body will be full of light. But if your eye is bad, your whole body will be full of darkness" (Matt. 6:22-23). Open doors are strongholds, areas of darkness that allow demons access into minds. Demons need consent when Jesus is in the picture, like they asked if they could go into the swine. Satan dwells in darkness, so dark places inside you allow him permission to hang around. If you're living in light, they have no invitation.

Solomon said, "Like a flitting sparrow, like a flying swallow, so a curse without cause shall not alight" (Prov. 26:2). If no cause (open door) exists, satan's curse can't enter. Remember the Exodus 15:26 scripture? God gave Moses a promise that none of what afflicted Israel's enemies would come on them, but that promise included a big word—*if*. Claiming freedom has requirements—the *ifs* of healing and demonic warfare. God's promises still apply and give freedom from the enemy but come with responsibility. You must listen to God's voice, do what's right in His sight, obey His commandments, and keep His statutes. *If* you do, you won't have diseases or demonic possessions. However, when you don't observe His expectations, you create open doors by your disobedience and willful sin. Israel, though a blessed nation, often became prey to enemies because they forgot God's *ifs* and were conquered (see Neh. 9:26-27). If your actions have allowed the devil access or you minister to someone else who has, you should clean the house and close the door on what allowed evil spirits in. That's accomplished by a simple concept— repentance. Coming to Him for forgiveness changes things.

After your physical and spiritual houses get cleaned out, your job is to stay free. Allowing the demonic back into your life means demons can return seven times worse (see Luke 11:26). Therefore, you should get away from whatever created the open door. After deliverance you're tender and weak and could still be susceptible to that demon's return, so you need time to grow stronger away from your own open door. Jesus showed another principle for the newly liberated. After his deliverance, the man who'd been possessed with legions asked Jesus if he could be one of His disciples. Jesus declined but said to proclaim His name. Though he could work for Jesus in a less-visible role, he wasn't ready for full-time ministry demands.

Jesus showed that plenty of jobs exist for people to work for the Lord. However, trying to take on disciples' responsibilities and tackle front-line, full-time jobs too soon may overwhelm those who are still weak from their experience. However, having a spirit at one time doesn't mean you won't eventually work in ministry. Some whom Jesus encountered were delivered and later contributed to His ministry in different ways. Mary Magdalene, for example, had seven devils cast from her (see Luke 8:2), but she ultimately became a great part of His ministry. She was even the first Jesus appeared to after His resurrection (see Mark 16:9). What if she hadn't been able to move forward but let her past control her present and her future wondrous walk with the Lord? She proved that eventually the formerly possessed can be a force for the Kingdom. How like the Lord to protect His weak ones for their destiny to come!

Unforgiveness

Open doors allow demonic entrance, so those doors should be closed. One opening is unforgiveness. Even the medical field has established a connection between unforgiveness and sickness because it keeps your body from going through its natural healing processes. Doctors have also discovered a relationship between chronic anxiety and unforgiveness. That constant worry produces substances that change your reactions to or willingness to take medications, which makes your body's normal sickness fighters unable to operate as they're intended.[4] Unforgiveness also impacts minds and bodies when you lose sleep as your mind churns. As you dwell on past hurts, the person about whom you're fretting is doing great, sleeping just fine. Unforgiveness, a sign of an unloving spirit, is one of satan's tools to keep you hurt and bound so you can't receive healing. In all you do, love should be your priority (see 1 John 4:7).

Unforgiveness acts like a block between you and God. I've heard this analogy: God wants to rain down blessings, but unforgiveness is an umbrella that keeps His blessings from hitting you. My friend Sylvia became sick, and doctors couldn't find the cause. This single mother of a young son became so sick she couldn't work, lost her job, and was unable to pay her bills. Finally, they diagnosed her with incurable lupus and gave her three months to survive. She lived a great distance from family, so she had no hope except the Lord. As she sought Him for healing, God revealed unforgiveness as the open door that allowed that satanic illness to come in. She prayed for His help to let go of wrongs another had inflicted upon her. When she forgave, gradually the lupus disappeared. She's still alive, watching her grandchildren grow up.

Allowing unforgiveness to enter creates an open door with legal access for the enemy. Left to grow, it becomes a root of bitterness, and roots and strongholds are harder to eliminate the longer they stay. After a miraculous healing, you may become sick again if you didn't get roots that allowed it in the first place. Forgiving is a choice, and letting go of past hurts is difficult. No matter who offends you, battles aren't against people but against satan and his hierarchy (see Eph. 6:12). It's spiritual warfare, even against sickness and unforgiveness. Battles you've fought and people who've lied about you, cheated on you, gossiped about you, made fun of you—it's a satanic battle. You must forgive your worst human enemy because humans aren't really your foes. While on the cross, Jesus forgave those who murdered Him (see Luke 23:34). That act was important to fulfilling His destiny.

When Jesus compared faith to a mustard seed, He said through faith, a mulberry tree's roots can be pulled up (see Luke 17:6). I like that He used the mulberry tree to compare with spiritual roots. That tree's roots grow easily, just by sticking a branch into the ground. Then, with watering, they grow fast, large, numerous, and deep. A mature tree bears frequent, bitter crops after it takes root.[5] Don't those descriptions sound like the enemy's roots? Roots of bitterness and other things are started easily, often from misunderstandings—maybe an innocent word that strikes you wrong. Perhaps a misinterpreted look or a hurt from being excluded. Maybe bad things you suffered—betrayal, abuse, insults, assaults. No matter how justified your hurt and anger may be, you must let it all go. Once you've allowed unforgiveness to fester, those roots grow large and fast, are bitter to the taste, and are difficult to remove. However, Jesus said those roots are hard to eliminate, but not impossible. Obedience to forgive despite my misgivings has changed my destiny more than once. By the way, when that branch dies, no matter how many times it's stuck into soil to make it grow, it won't!

Unforgiveness is difficult to overcome, but a good way is to pray for your enemies. That's hard; but Jesus said, "Whenever you stand praying, if you have anything against anyone, forgive him, that your Father in heaven may also forgive you your trespasses" (Mark 11:25). That's simply stated, but how profound that forgiving should be part of your daily prayer life and crucial to getting answered prayers. When Abraham met Abimelech, whom he perceived as a threat, he said Sarah was his sister. After Abimelech took Sarah to become his wife, his other wives became barren. Abraham prayed for Abimelech, his wives, and the female servants' barrenness. Not only did God take infertility from Abimelech's wives; in the next chapter, Sarah conceived and Isaac was born (see Gen. 20:2, 17-18; 21:2). Paul said to overcome evil by good (see Rom. 12:21). Praying for your enemies is a good thing and puts forgiveness into action while opening the way for God to pour blessings on you.

Others

Other common open doors allow demonic access. In Chapter Seven, I talked about fear as a block to healing. It's also a huge open door that allows the enemy's entrance. Also, mind-altering substances like illegal or even some legal drugs can make your mind susceptible to evil intrusions. Hypnosis turns your will over to someone else as you allow your mind to be modified. Another frequent open door is from past or present sexual sins. That often invites a lust spirit, and many have come to us for deliverance from that. That spirit is so blatant that more than once, I've perceived it on someone just by glancing at him/her. Sexual spirits are rampant throughout the world as escalating accounts of deviant actions flood the news. Even some Christians allow open doors of perversion into their bodies, minds, and homes as they dabble in pornography. Some think these are victimless activities, but this open door makes way for demonic oppression or possession for those participants and often their exposed children. David's life teaches that when your eye lingers where it shouldn't, tragic consequences follow you and your family (see 2 Sam. 11:2). These open doors should be closed and soul ties from past liaisons broken, even if the perversion occurred through rape or molestation.

Another open door is exposure to the occult. When someone dabbles in it, that's satan's territory. Paul warned to "give [no] place to the devil" (Eph. 4:27); that includes open doors, especially right in his house. If you enter the enemy's territory, you're not just inviting him in but waving your arms to welcome him. The Bible refers several times to spirits associated with the occult. A spirit of divination, mediums, and familiar spirits are mentioned (see Acts 16:16; Lev. 20:27). Although Saul had "put the mediums and the spiritists out of the land" (1 Sam. 28:3), when he grew fearful during war with the Philistines, he panicked. He hadn't heard from God, so he asked the witch of En Dor for a séance with Samuel, who was dead. Samuel said that because of his disobedience, unfaithfulness, and guidance from a medium, Saul and his sons would die the next day (see 1 Sam. 28:5, 8, 18-19; 1 Chron. 10:13). It came to pass.

After people saw Holy Spirit's power on first century disciples, they knew they needed to get rid of items tied to the devil and the demonic realm. Those who practiced the occult burned their books at a great financial sacrifice—50,000 pieces of silver (see Acts 19:19). That should be a lesson. Playing with the occult in any way is dangerous. Many of these activities don't seem wrong and perhaps you've done them unwittingly—horoscopes, fortunetellers, séances, Ouija boards, tarot cards, Magic 8 balls, or others. Once, we went to the home of a Christian couple with a young child who was having nightmares and showing aggression. The school psychologist had told them their son needed therapy; but they trusted the Lord, not a psychiatrist. Upon entering his room, I felt an evil spirit, so I surveyed the room. Ungodly movies with vampires and wizards filled his shelves, and Pokémon cards were scattered around. When we told them how spirits are associated with those, they immediately threw them away. We prayed, and their boy was healed.

Deliverance is essential, but beware. Before exorcising a demon, make sure that person doesn't retain open doors that will attract more demons when current ones leave. I've said this before, but it's worth repeating. If you pray for the demon's release from that person's body or home and he/she still operates with open doors, those demons and worse will return (see Matt. 12:45). Once, a woman came for deliverance because evil spirits had become so blatant in her house that they visually appeared. As we talked, she sobbed about implications for her family. Though we felt compassion, her conversation let us know one thing—we shouldn't conduct deliverance because she and her husband were unsaved. She wasn't sure if she wanted to be saved, so we told her they both needed to think hard about the most important decision they'd ever make. We knew a pastor was visiting her the next day and could lead them in that prayer she was unwilling to speak that day. Both she and her husband were saved and delivered, and their home was cleansed.

Conclusion

Several years ago, I was on the altar team at mid-week service when a young lady approached. As I usually do, I closed my eyes and took her hands. I started to tell her I felt the Spirit but immediately realized what I felt wasn't Holy Spirit. I opened my eyes and saw demons manifesting—foaming at the mouth and an intense, hate-filled stare. I was taken aback; then manifestations became more pronounced. I'd been in deliverance services since childhood and had personally been involved in multiple deliverances, but I was unprepared for that intensity. That night, I should've shown up ministry-ready. We later spent much personal time with that lovely woman who wanted freedom from what had infested her life and body.

Demons are a reality in a Christian walk. They oppress and possess others and afflict many with mental and physical maladies. As a person with a deliverance ministry, you should be spiritually in tune so you recognize those spirits. The Bible has much to say about evil spirits, and Jesus' ministry gives examples for recognizing and overcoming them. After He healed the demon-possessed man, people were frightened. They knew a problem existed because they'd ineffectively tried to restrain the man; but they were more at ease with the demonic than with Jesus, so they asked Him to leave. Many today know this world is filled with evil but have grown used to the demonic rather than Jesus and His freedom. John says it perfectly: "Men loved darkness rather than light, because their deeds were evil" (John 3:19). Most people aren't comfortable talking about deliverance, let alone ministering to one who needs to be freed. Because of sin and fear, people may shun you as you take authority over demons, but where else can those who are bound find deliverance? By closing doors that have been opened and then repenting, the oppressed/possessed can be freed and stay freed. Walk cautiously in deliverance and test the spirits to be wise as well as authoritative. Then know those spirits have to obey.

Questions to Ponder

Answers in the Appendix

1   a.   What are two ways a person can be afflicted by demons?

     b.   Describe behaviors that demonstrated possession in the man/men at the Gadarenes and the demon-possessed boy.

     c.   Is it necessary to know the name of a demon in order to cast it out?

     d.   Which gift should you apply when you don't know whom to trust?

2   a.   Give examples of sicknesses attributed to many causes that can actually be demonic possession.

     b.   The word for *seize* or *convulse* has a violent connotation. Give some of the violent things these demons did.

     c.   Give emotional/psychological illnesses which the Bible attributes to demons.

     d.   How do Judas and other biblical stories show suicide's cause to be demons?

3   a.   Besides Jesus' ministry, give other evil spirits listed in the Bible.

     b.   What are good spirits operating in the earth?

     c.   Tell Job's friend's description of how he perceived a demon's presence. Have you experienced this sensation?

4   a.   What's an open door?

     b.   Fill in the blanks: "God's ___ come with ___."

     c.   How do you close open doors?

     d.   Why should you wait a while after deliverance before doing front-line work for the Lord?

e. Does having a demon at one time mean you can never work for the Lord?

5 a. How does the medical field connect unforgiveness and sickness?

b. Give the analogy of how unforgiveness works to keep you sick.

c. Left to grow, unforgiveness becomes a root of what?

d. How does Jesus' story of the mulberry tree compare to spiritual roots?

e. Fill in the blanks: "Unforgiveness is ___ to ___, but a good ___ is to ___ for your ___.

f. How did God reward Abraham for praying for his enemy?

6 a. Give other open doors from this chapter that can allow demonic oppression or possession.

b. Why is dabbling in the occult dangerous?

c. Name some seemingly innocent open doors associated with the occult.

d. Why should you refuse to deliver some who approach you?

DISCUSSION: What stands out to you about the deliverance Jesus performed with the man with the legions of demons and the possessed son?

Chapter Ten

Relationship

RELATIONSHIP WITH THE FATHER COMES FROM TIME WITH HIM, and healings often occur during that time. One night I attended one of our services despite being in great pain from a groin and knee injury. Sitting was less painful than standing, so I stayed seated as much as possible but finally stood when worship began. To lean against something, I went forward and braced my legs against the altar. That night as I stood before Him, He also stood before me. During worship, I felt an intense presence surround me. As I looked up, I became immersed in the wonder of His presence as worship consumed us. By the time I walked away, all pain was gone and never returned. Practicing relationship with the Father brings many blessings, including healing.

Often I hear people say they know God. That's a wonderful but a broad and relative statement. On some level, it's true for all Christians. They've accepted Jesus as Savior. They pray. They go to church; however, if church is all you know about God, you're not in an intimate relationship with Him. A difference exists between salvation and intimacy, between religion and relationship. After you personally know God and His character, you understand that no matter what happens, He has your back. Through relationship, you know Him as more than an "I-know-He-can-but-will-He?" God. With relationship, without hesitation, you can say, "Yes, He will." Relationship makes a tremendous difference.

What Did Jesus Do?

Before word of Lazarus' illness, Jesus had already become aware of His own life being in danger. As a result, He didn't remain in Judea but stayed beyond the Jordan where He performed signs and wonders (see John 11:1-46; 10:40-42). Then Lazarus' sisters sent word that he had become ill. Instead of leaving immediately to heal His good friend, He said Lazarus wouldn't die from the sickness but that the scenario would be for God's glory (see John 11:4). As a matter of fact, He waited two more days to go to Lazarus. When He decided to return, disciples discouraged Him because of threats to Him (see John 11:8). Jesus reminded them He had much to do while He could, a reference to His future passing. He told them Lazarus was sleeping, so He must awaken him. They misunderstood and said sleep would aid in Lazarus' healing. Then Jesus clarified and told them Lazarus had already died, and He was glad He hadn't been there because they needed to believe. Thomas alluded to the danger if Jesus returned to Judea by saying they should go and die with Him (see John 11:16).

By the time He arrived at Bethany, his friend had been in the tomb four days. As He approached the sisters' house, many of their friends were grieving. Someone saw Him coming and told Martha. She met Him outside of town while Mary continued to sit at the house. Martha told Him if He'd been there, Lazarus wouldn't have died. Then she said she knew if He asked, God would give Him anything. However, though she declared faith in His ability to have avoided Lazarus' death and now for a resurrection, when the Lord answered that Lazarus would rise again, she showed her actual unbelief. She misunderstood His meaning and thought He was talking about the latter-day resurrection. As Jesus taught her, she affirmed her belief in Him (see John 11:21-27).

Then Martha left and privately told Mary that Jesus was calling her. Her comforting friends saw her leave quickly, so they followed and assumed she was going to the tomb to mourn. Instead, she went to the Master. As she saw Him, she fell at His feet and spoke the same words Martha had said (see John 11:21, 32). However, instead of answering her statement with doctrine like He had with Martha, Jesus reacted to her and her friends' mourning. He "groaned in the spirit and was troubled" (John 11:33) and asked where the body was laid. As they told Him to come with them, He wept (see John 11:35). Those around commented about His love for Lazarus, but some criticized His not coming earlier to avoid Lazarus' death. Jesus didn't respond but again groaned as He approached the tomb, a cave with a stone in the doorway.

When Jesus commanded them to remove the stone, Martha commented that Lazarus had been entombed four days and would surely stink (see John 11:39). Jesus said He'd already told her if she believed, she'd see God's glory. She acquiesced, and they removed it from the entrance. Jesus then prayed, "Father, I thank You that You have heard Me. And I know that You always hear Me, but because of the people who are standing by I said this, that they may believe that You sent Me" (John 11:41-42). Then, He cried loudly, "Lazarus, come forth!" (John 11:43). In response to Jesus' command, Lazarus bounded from his tomb, wrapped from head to toe with grave clothes. Jesus told them to take those clothes off. After this, Mary's friends believed on Jesus, but others reported the miracle to the Pharisees.

Knowing Jesus

Lazarus' story is a sweet, powerful picture of knowing Jesus. Though this isn't the only reference to this family (see Matt. 26:2; Mark 14:3-9; Luke 10:38-42), this gospel alone tells about Lazarus' resurrection. These siblings from Bethany, a small town two miles east of Jerusalem, had formed a relationship with Jesus. Two sisters and their brother—Martha, Mary, and Lazarus—all loved Him dearly; and He loved them, too. He had stayed with them often while He was in the area, having dinner and resting at their house from time to time. He'd later visit here the week before His crucifixion (see John 12:1). The relationship between Jesus and this family should speak about your own relationship with Him. Intimacy means not just being acquainted with someone but spending time with that person. Through exposure, you get to know each other's characters, habits, personalities, godly walks, idiosyncrasies. Jesus knew them as friends; and they knew Him that way, too. Because of relationship, when the dead Lazarus heard Jesus' voice calling him, he recognized it and responded. That familiar voice spoke life into his body.

Biblical saints demonstrate the concept of relationship. Elijah intimately knew the widow and her son with whom he lived for three years. Elisha had stayed at the Shunammite woman's house and partaken of her hospitality (see 1 Kings 17:10-24; 2 Kings 4:8-11). These stories show an important concept. Matthew states how seeking relationship and helping the prophet bring rewards: "He who receives a prophet in the name of a prophet shall receive a prophet's reward. And he who receives a righteous man in the name of a righteous man shall receive a righteous man's reward" (Matt. 10:41). The Lord wants His workers cared for—His prophets, ministers, leaders, pastors, and righteous men. If you do, expect His blessings. Too many come to Jesus for their prophet's reward but haven't sown into Him. Though she and her son were starving, the widow gave Elijah a cake first and then a home during the drought. Her reward—multiplication of food and resurrection of her son. The Shunammite woman built and furnished a room for whenever Elisha passed by. Her reward—a baby then a resurrection when that baby died. Lazarus and his sisters befriended, fed, loved, and welcomed Jesus into their home to rest and recharge. Their reward—a resurrection. Relationship has rewards, even resurrecting that which is dead.

Glorifying God

Relationship with the Father makes you desire all things to be for His glory. When Jesus taught about asking in His name, He specified that it must be to glorify God (see John 14:13). As Jesus and the disciples were returning to heal Lazarus, He commented on the miracle's purpose. He was glad He hadn't been there when Lazarus died so they'd believe (see John 11:15). Jesus wanted God to receive the glory and knew if He were there, Lazarus would've been healed. What a message! When Jesus comes around, healing follows. Although His healings were mighty and many, they had a greater purpose—to glorify God. Once, a great crowd converged on Him at the mountain by the Sea of Galilee and brought the lame, blind, mute, maimed, and others and "laid them down at Jesus' feet" (Matt. 15:30). After they were healed, the crowd marveled at the miracles and glorified God (see Matt. 15:31). This Greek word for *glorified* is *doxazo,* from *doxa,* "glory (as very apparent)...honour, praise, worship."[1] God must get glory because it's all about Him.

Peter says that everyone who ministers should do so with God's ability and for His glory through Jesus (see 1 Pet. 4:11). Jesus showed how His actions were for God's glory through Lazarus' resurrection. After Jesus first heard of the illness, He commented that the sickness wasn't about Lazarus' death but God's glory and His Son's validation. He also told Martha she'd see God's glory (see John 11:4, 40). Both used *doxa.* At the tomb He again showed His honor of God by saying He knew God had always heard Him but was praying so those around would know He was sent by the Father (see John 11:42). Later after the triumphal entry, Jesus reiterated His purpose for coming to earth and dying on the cross. He said, "Father, glorify Your name" (John 12:28). The Father spoke audibly that He had glorified it and would again. As you obey God's will, He glorifies Himself through you.

During this exchange with His Father, Jesus was facing a dreaded ordeal, but He willingly obeyed so the Father would be glorified. This should make you check your motivations. If you're doing God's work for any reason except to bring Him glory, you're wrong. Also, often people neglect to give Him honor for His miracle and healing powers and credit other explanations—doctors, medicines, mistaken diagnoses. Sometimes He reveals an upcoming pitfall that's avoided; when it doesn't happen, some say they must've been mistaken or the situation just worked out. God deserves the glory for everything. He may allow dire events to happen so He can work in the situation, and others will know definitively that He is Lord. Lazarus' death and resurrection left no room to credit anything but God. Raising someone who's in the tomb four days isn't a matter of something just working out. This was all God, who wants to be glorified.

Obeying God's Will

Because of relationship, Jesus' decisions were determined by His Father; this story is an example of how He sought God. He delayed His trip then returned to Bethany not just because of His desire to help a friend but because God had ordained the time and purpose. His human side would've rushed back to heal His friend, but He did it how God wanted. Other great men also did God's will. Elijah called drought at God's word. Then at the sacrifice, he said, "I am Your servant, and...I have done all things at Your word" (1 Kings 18:36). The second part of your seeking God's will is obeying, a principle emphasized throughout this book. If you love Him, you keep His commandments (see John 14:15).

Lazarus' sister Mary, as a sinner, knew how the Lord had changed her, so she adored and eagerly obeyed Him. After Lazarus died, when she heard Jesus had arrived, Martha left to meet Him. She didn't understand that obedience often means awaiting His call *then* acting with willingness. After she left Him, she secretly told Mary, "The Teacher has come and is calling for you" (see John 11:28). When Jesus was *calling* Mary, that word was *phoneo* "to address in words or by name."[2] How awesome when Jesus knows you intimately enough to call you by name. Mary awaited His call before she moved then hastened to Him. Like Jesus with His Father, when you have relationship, you know to move or to stay because you're in tune with His leading, not your own thoughts.

After He summoned her, she then "rose up quickly" (see John 11:31). *Quickly* is *tacheos*, "speedily...suddenly."[3] Obedience involves many aspects, and one is speedy response. Are you missing blessings like healings because you aren't swift to obey? Often breakthrough comes as you couple faith with unquestioning, immediate obedience even if you don't understand. Like disciples didn't comprehend that Jesus' comment about Lazarus' sleeping was really telling about Lazarus' death, people today misunderstand God's plan or Jesus' words. Hesitation indicates lack of faith and trust in Him.

The Bible speaks frequently about obedience, even when what God spoke seemed silly. God uses the "foolish things of the world to put to shame the wise" (1 Cor. 1:27), like rolling away a stone from a tomb that obviously has a stench. Naaman procured healing through foolish obedience. He was a Syrian officer with leprosy, a disease that made even upstanding folks become social pariahs. Then, Elisha said to dip seven times in Jordan, an order that angered Naaman. The Jordan was dirty, and better rivers were available. When he balked, his servants told him that if the prophet had asked Naaman to do anything else, he would have gladly obeyed. Despite this undesirable and foolish prophetic word, he should answer the Lord's call exactly. He did and was healed (see 2 Kings

5:1-14). Doing things God's way creates results. If God nudges your heart to minister to someone or someone ministers to you, you should be ready, willing, and swiftly obedient. God has victory, and immediate obedience to His will is the key.

The Backlash

Relationship's results often make you a target. Lazarus' resurrection prompted varied responses from Jews. Mary's visitors saw this miracle and turned to Jesus. How appropriate that her friends who'd seen her relationship with the Master believed as a result of the resurrection. Intense relationship draws others to Him. Some people, though, still didn't see His deity and reported the resurrection to furious Pharisees, who were plotting to kill Him because His signs and wonders created more trust in this Man's rhetoric. If a larger number believed Him, their plan could be endangered. Even many rulers believed but didn't confess because they'd be driven from the temple (see John 12:42). Because of those lying in wait, Jesus avoided Jews who wanted Him dead. He left to stay in a city near the wilderness.

Meanwhile, people gathered in Jerusalem for Passover and wondered if they'd see this Miracle Worker during the holiday. Despite or because of His popularity, the chief priests and Pharisees gave a command that anyone who knew Jesus' whereabouts should report it so they could seize Him (see John 11:57). Then, about a week before Passover, Jesus returned to Bethany to spend time with friends. There, He wasn't the only target of Jewish leaders; they also wanted to kill Lazarus. Word had gotten around about the resurrection, so Lazarus had become famous. Tourists went to Bethany to see the Miracle Worker as well as the miracle. As a result, they believed in Jesus. Just because Lazarus was alive, church leaders hated him; his very life testified of Jesus, and they wanted to eliminate both (see John 12:9-11). When you have relationship with Jesus and experience His blessings, you're a target. However, Jesus tells you not to worry because the world hated Him before it hated you (see John 15:18). The two siblings, Mary (for her intimacy) and Lazarus (for his life), brought the lost to the Lord. Does your life draw others, too?

To Serve Jesus

The word *serve* in your Christian walk means many things. Serving the Lord by attending church, helping others, or paying tithes is wonderful and important, but serving encompasses much more. The sisters show a difference in their perceptions about how to serve Him. Once, the family had company, including Jesus. Think of that! Jesus was sitting in their house, eating their food, teaching the Word, laughing with them. However, instead of seeing the wonder and rejoicing about His presence in her home, Martha fretted about her overload of work. Because her sister wasn't serving like Martha did but rather was learning from Jesus, she felt Mary was shirking her duty to help prepare and serve His dinner. She scolded Jesus for not making Mary help (see Luke 10:38-42). Many love, know, and serve Him; but like Martha, their serving neglects the fullness of experiencing Him!

God has given each of us one or more motivational gifts—prophecy, ministry, teaching, exhorting, giving, leading, mercy (see Rom. 12:6-8). He provides these individual gifts according to our personalities, experiences, educations, or interests to enhance our lives and work for His Kingdom. These gifts are part of our characters, our DNA, whether using them in daily life or for ministry. The NIV uses the word, "serving," instead of "ministry" as one of the gifts. Martha's personality was to serve, and she obviously used that gift well. While others fellowshipped with the Lord, she served because that was who she was. What a wonderful, necessary gift! However, Martha missed the point of relationship. No matter which gift defines you, you're not to neglect other aspects of your service to Him, especially fostering intimacy. It's more than just head knowledge, and serving Him isn't to be drudgery.

Many get so caught up in the minutiae of day-to-day life or even ministry that they fail to see a bigger picture of serving Jesus—the beauty of His presence. Too often, you become consumed by responsibilities— in the house, with the kids, at your job. Then, even what you do for the Lord becomes an onerous chore. If your attitude changes from gladness to resentment, you should reevaluate what you do. Your gifts are treasures; but if they become obligations or take precedence over intimate time with the Master, you miss a precious opportunity to know Him more. Martha shows not to get so caught up in doing *good* things for Jesus that you aren't doing *God* things.

After she scolded Him, Jesus didn't reprimand Mary but rather told Martha not to worry about what was secondary in life's priorities. He expressed that Mary had chosen what wouldn't be taken from her (see Luke 10:42). That counsel was great, but Martha didn't change. Six days before Passover, Jesus again returned to Bethany. No one knew then how few days He had left on earth and what an honor that He'd chosen to spend the bulk of His time with this family. While He was there, "they made Him a supper; and Martha served" (John 12:2). Again, Martha chose to serve despite her resurrected brother sitting there rubbing elbows with the Healer and Jesus' telling her to choose the good things like Mary. Mary had grown more in love with Him, but Martha stopped short of intimacy by keeping her pattern of how to serve Jesus. Are you a Martha or a Mary? How often do you take your time with Him for granted? Is Jesus beckoning you to grow closer to Him, set your religion aside, and serve Him through deeper relationship?

Religion: Martha

Both Martha and Mary knew the Lord but are examples of the difference between religion and relationship. Most Christians are Marthas who do serve Him, but they know him on a formal rather than intimate level. They serve through their works, their own way, or their past practices, not seeking a deeper *now* walk with Him. Martha's attitude and comments directed toward Jesus show how religion operates. Like Martha, religion finds fault when He does things differently from how they think it should be done. First, she complained to Him about Mary's not helping. Later, when Lazarus died, Martha and others criticized Him by saying He should've come sooner. After He asked them to take the stone from the tomb, Martha argued because of the stench from Lazarus' decaying body (see John 11:21, 37, 39). If you presume to know what Jesus should do and how He should do it better than He does, you're operating in religion. If you believe your calling is to criticize Jesus, your pastor, or others in the ministry, you should rethink. You're probably a Martha who thought Jesus needed her advice.

Religion doesn't get beyond doctrine. Many serve Jesus, believe He's the Son of God, and know the rhetoric. After Martha told Jesus that if He'd been there, the death wouldn't have happened, she added that she knew even then that whatever He asked God, God would do. When Jesus told Martha that Lazarus would rise, she couldn't conceive of His boundless ability to raise her brother. She affirmed with doctrinal head knowledge that her brother would rise in the resurrection. She also voiced that He *could* raise Lazarus, but she didn't truly believe it and couldn't comprehend what He was telling her. That's religion, based on doctrine rather than relationship.

Religion pays lip service to healing but doesn't truly believe (see John 11:22-24). They assert that miracles *could* happen because they don't have relationship to know they *will* happen. If called upon to believe in His healing and miracle character, they have no substance or experience to believe He *can* do anything. Jesus trusted God's ability because He came from a familiarity stance and not just theoretical knowledge of God's abilities. He could speak with power and authority because He'd seen firsthand what God could do. After you've witnessed God's power for yourself, you can authoritatively believe and speak. Martha's time had been spent serving instead of learning about Him. Think of that! She had an opportunity that people for all of time would have loved—to experience the Lord personally—His scent, His voice, His touch, His smile, His footsteps. How sad that Martha took His presence for granted and after all her days with Jesus still remained at the salvation message. Doesn't that sound like modern-day religion?

Thomas' comments also show religion, not relationship. He too should've had a close, intimate relationship with Him. As one of His twelve, Thomas knew Him well. However, he was the doubter who later wouldn't believe the resurrected Jesus until he felt the scars (see John 20:25). His words were faith's opposite and demonstrate most of today's religion. Thomas wouldn't believe until he saw, while faith is believing *before* you see. Jesus said to him, "Because you have seen Me, you have believed. Blessed are those who have not seen and yet have believed" (John 20:29). Then, before they left to raise Lazarus, Thomas fretted about Jesus' going because He would probably be killed by Pharisees. His comment, perhaps sarcastically, about dying with Jesus shows his knowledge of Jesus but lack of deep relationship (see John 11:16). Like Martha, he didn't truly understand or believe that Jesus could do such extraordinary feats as resurrecting a man in the tomb four days or that Jesus Himself would rise.

Pharisees were the ultimate religious people, concerned about keeping Jesus from infecting parishioners. They were men educated and chosen to do God's work but were so out of touch with Him that they plotted His own Son's death. How ironic they were praying for Messiah to arrive while scheming to kill Him. In a few days, that Messiah would come riding into town on a donkey (see Mark 11:1-11), but they were too steeped in their religious ways and concern about safeguarding their temple businesses to see truth when Truth arrived. Then, they'd hang Him on a tree, which He had created. Religion stops before relationship. Jesus wants intimacy, not just head knowledge and doctrine. Religion has "a form of godliness but den[ies] its power [*dunamis*]" (2 Tim. 3:5). As a result, religion lacks power.

Relationship: Mary

Mary, on the other hand, demonstrates relationship. I've heard the difference between the sisters described this way: Martha held her hands out; Mary held her hands up. Before Jesus went to resurrect Lazarus, He was told, "He whom You love is sick" (John 11:3). If you have relationship, others recognize that. After He said they were going to heal Lazarus, Scripture says, "Jesus loved Martha and her sister and Lazarus" (John 11:5). Jesus knew and loved them all, but a difference existed in His relationship with each. The dissimilarity between the sisters had been apparent when Jesus visited their house. "Martha was distracted with much serving" while Mary sat at His feet and listened to the Word (see Luke 10:39-40). Later, the difference would also be obvious when Mary would again sit at His feet, Lazarus would be with Him at the table, and Martha would again serve (see John 12:2-3). Like Mary sought Him with everything in her, you should pursue Him also. Changing from the Martha persona into Mary, you become more in love with the Lord. Mary adored and trusted Him implicitly because she'd gone beyond initial experience and into a relational one. Relationship brings what simple knowledge doesn't.

The gospels describe a woman who attended a gathering and anointed Jesus. Some references (see Matt. 26:7; Mark 14:3-9) don't name the woman but depict the event at Simon's house. Many believe this unnamed woman wasn't Mary of Bethany. However, evidence says this anointing scene is the same one described after Lazarus' resurrection, and it "was that Mary who anointed the Lord" (John 11:2). Luke tells about the unnamed woman and calls her "a sinner" (Luke 7:37). She was so bad that Simon silently criticized Jesus for allowing her to attend. Mary ignored what others said about her because she had a purpose—to approach Jesus with her sacrifice. Though others condemned her as unworthy, Mary personified Jesus' past teachings about the importance of what's inside a person rather than what others see (see Matt. 23:28). She had a past that wasn't pretty but possessed a beautiful spirit. Today, people condemn many aspects of others, including past indiscretions, lack of spiritual discernment, or worship of the Lord. If you're a God-pleaser, others' opinions of your Christian walk won't matter.

John records the anointing ceremony and says Judas, the ministry treasurer, disapproved of her wasting precious spices that could've been sold to help the poor (see John 12:3-8). While Mary took advantage of her time with the Lord, the Pharisee Simon, thieving Judas, and serving Martha found fault. Seeking relationship rather than religion produces intimacy and results. As Martha and Mary approached Him after Lazarus died, they said the same statement: "Lord, if You had been here, my brother would not have died" (see John 11:21, 32). Their words were the same, but their degrees of intimacy elicited different responses from Jesus. Martha received a doctrine lesson about the resurrection. Mary *got* a resurrection. With relationship, He responds. The nearer you draw to Him, the more relationship you have and the more you'll please Him. Then, watch the healing results.

Worship

I love this subject, so how appropriate that my book's last section deals with worship! The more time you spend with someone, the more you grow to know each other. With God, that time comes by praying, being in His Word, praising, and worshiping. You should go to Him regularly and not with an agenda except being with Him. Paul says, "Let us continually offer the sacrifice of praise to God, that is, the fruit of our lips, giving thanks to His name" (Heb. 13:15). Constant worship brings you into His presence; then His presence changes everything. Romans 12:1 instructs you about your Christian walk: "I beseech you...[to] present your bodies a living sacrifice, holy, acceptable to God, which is your reasonable service." I've quoted this scripture before because many lessons may be gleaned from the words' meanings. Here, Paul says sacrificing your bodies, giving all, is your "reasonable service." The word he used for *service* is *latreia*, and one meaning is "worship."[4] Presenting yourself wholly to Him is your worship, your reasonable service.

Martha sacrificed by serving Jesus, but Mary served also and gained intimacy as her worship became her sacrifice. Some desire what He gives, like a healing, but Mary wanted the *Healer*. When she boldly fell at His feet to speak about her brother (see John 11:32), those actions were worship. Later, when Jesus again came to their house, Mary's adoration was even more intense and loving. She gave what was precious—spices, love, humility, reputation. Worship requires sacrifice; and you humbly give all, no matter the cost. Mary's worship was honest, intense, lavish, and necessary. Although Martha's serving was her concept of hospitality to the Lord, Jesus explained to critics as Mary washed His dusty feet that *she* truly exemplified hospitality. Though her actions were in preparation for His death, Matthew said what she did would memorialize her (see John 12:3, 7-8; Matt. 26:13). Wow! Mary has been alluded to billions of times because of her relationship with the Lord. Worship was the key.

With her long, dark hair falling across her olive cheeks, she unpretentiously knelt to rub ointment on her Love's feet. Luke says she washed His feet with her tears, dried them with her hair, kissed them, and anointed them with oil (see Luke 7:38). Matthew and Mark say she poured the oil on His head (see Matt. 26:7; Mark 14:3). Though others criticized her for wasting expensive oil and condemned Jesus for not knowing her reputation, she wasn't dissuaded from worship. She took that pound of costly oil of spikenard, broke the flask, and poured it on Him. When she did, worship's fragrance filled the house (see John 12:3). Probably days later, the scent of her worship still lingered in her hair, like it does as your worship time with the Lord carries you through days to come. Your sacrifice of worship poured on Him permeates the whole place, especially your house, your body of flesh (see 2 Cor. 5:1). Although her worship was for Him alone, naysayers were also beneficiaries of her anointing. What kind of fragrance does your time with Him exude?

Others in the Bible knew worship's importance. David was the quintessential worshiper. Unlike Martha who ignored Jesus' instructions when He said she needed just "one thing" (Luke 10:42), David was considered a man who desired that "One thing"—to dwell in God's house (Ps. 27:4). Instead of following Saul's model of not bringing God's presence back during his reign, when David became king, his priority was to bring the ark to Jerusalem. That involved the entire nation worshiping with great pomp and circumstance, dancing and shouting. Then, he created a tabernacle with continuous worship (see 2 Sam. 6; 1 Chron. 16:37, 40). His obsession with God's presence made him known as a man after God's heart (see Acts 13:22). The psalmist said to "Offer to God thanksgiving, and pay your vows to the Most High. Call upon Me in the day of trouble; I will deliver you, and you shall glorify Me" (Ps. 50:14-15). Doesn't that promise thrill you? Worship is the pathway to call upon the Lord when trouble comes.

Worship is also crucial to warfare and sends demons running (see 1 Sam. 16:23). Jehoshaphat warred against three armies in an unwinnable battle. God spoke through the prophet that he wouldn't need to fight the battle but would witness the Lord's salvation (see 2 Chron. 20:17). The prophet told the army to stand still and watch the Lord fight. Then, Jehoshaphat and all Jerusalem bowed before the Lord and sang praises with "voices loud and high" (2 Chron. 20:19). They knew God was their hope, so they worshiped with abandon like David had danced on his trip back to Jerusalem. Jehoshaphat's worshipers praised before the battle and preceded the army. They didn't have to fight because God took over and created confusion among their enemies, who killed each other. Judah won a resounding victory (see 2 Chron. 20:21-23). If you're surrounded on all sides by innumerable enemies, worship brings confusion to the enemy. Instead of defeat, they gathered the wealth of the wicked. It's stored up and awaiting the righteous with relationship (see Prov. 13:22).

Worship permeated Jesus' healing stories. The Syro-Phoenician woman worshiped, He listened, and He healed her daughter. A leper fell on his face in worship before Jesus healed him (see Matt. 15:21-28; 8:1-4). After he saw Jesus, Jairus fell at the Master's feet and worshiped Him (see Mark 5:22). The lady with the issue of blood fell and worshiped even before Jesus pronounced her healed (see Mark 5:22; Luke 8:47). After the ten lepers were cleansed, one returned, glorified God with a loud voice, fell on his face, gave Jesus thanks, and worshiped as he followed Jesus (see Luke 17:15-16). Worship is so important that when the Pharisees criticized His disciples' loud praises, Jesus told them that if they didn't worship him, the rocks would (see Luke 19:37-40).

Bartimaeus' story is also about worship. Because of His amazing miracles, Jesus' reputation had preceded Him before He met Bartimaeus. As He approached the Lord, Bartimaeus called His name and worshiped, saying "Rabboni" (see Mark 10:51), meaning, "My Great One."[5] Miracles elicit worship, which draws the lost, and Jesus is all about people—their healing as well as their salvation. Healing is a wonderful testimony that speaks of God's love, so those who witnessed Bartimaeus' miracle praised the Lord. However, Bartimaeus worshiped *before* he received the miracle. You don't worship because you want things, but you get things because you worship. Desperation attracts the Lord's attention, but pairing desperation with faith and worship opens the way to *dunamis'* healing power. The psalmist said, "Let everything that has breath praise the Lord" (Ps. 150:6). If you're still breathing, praise Him.

Conclusion

Even though your relationship puts you on the front line of enemy fire because you waste precious spices on Him or because you're a walking miracle, relationship matters. The Lord uses many things to heal; one is worship, a magnet that draws Holy Spirit. Obedience matters, too. After my surgery, my strength level was very low. The Lord impressed me to ask our pastor to anoint those needing extreme strength. The next Sunday, he announced that after church he'd pray for us in the fellowship room. A large group gathered for his and the elders' prayers. As he laid hands on me, I felt something go into my body. The next week, I couldn't believe the difference in my energy, and it got better each day until I was back to normal. Obedience to do His will His way made the difference, then and now, and I have plenty of strength for my life and ministry demands.

Most Christians have put God into a box made of walls of what He *can* do but not what He *will* do. They serve Him without personal, intimate relationship. You can serve by doing, but serving by loving is His way. When Jesus wanted to take the stone from the tomb, Martha reminded Him that Lazarus had already been dead four days, so the stench would be significant. Stinking situations aren't too hard for Jesus. Death sentences and death itself aren't too hard for Jesus. As Lazarus burst from the tomb, Jesus ordered His grave clothes taken off him. He wants to remove what's stinking and binds you. As you seek relationship instead of just religion, you should arise from your coffin of defeat because God's able to do great things. Relationship with Jesus is power.

Questions to Ponder

Answers in the Appendix

1   a.   How did this family get to know Jesus better?

     b.   Why is spending time with someone important?

     c.   Explain "prophet's reward."

     d.   Give examples of that from Scripture.

2   a.   What principles can you glean from Jesus' saying He was glad He wasn't there when Lazarus died?

     b.   Fill in the blanks: "As you ___ God's ___, He ___ ___ through you."

     c.   How was Lazarus' resurrection an undeniable miracle?

3   a.   How did Jesus' return to Bethany demonstrate His doing God's will?

     b.   Show how Mary's response to the Lord's call exhibited obedience.

     c.   Explain how God uses the world's foolish things.

4   a.   What were the varied reactions to Lazarus' resurrection?

     b.   Why were people seeking to kill both Lazarus and Jesus? How might that situation occur today?

5   a.   Explain different ways you can serve the Lord.

     b.   How did Martha serve Him? How did Mary?

     c.   How do you know Martha didn't change after Jesus told her to choose what wouldn't be taken from her?

6   a.   What's the difference between religion and relationship?

     b.   How do the sisters represent each of these?

     c.   Describe how Martha represents religion.

d. How do Thomas and the Pharisees also demonstrate religion?

7 a. Give one way you can foster relationship.

b. Fill in the blanks: "If you have ___, others ___ that."

c. Give evidence that Lazarus' sister Mary was the sinner whom Simon criticized.

d. What did Mary's relationship accomplish that Martha's religion did not?

8 a. What does Romans 12:1 teach about worship?

b. How did Mary exemplify hospitality?

c. Describe the anointing scene.

d. How did Martha's "one thing" differ from David's?

e. Tell the story of how worship brought victory to Jehoshaphat.

f. Give examples of people who worshiped Jesus as part of their healing.

g. Fill in the blanks: "You don't ___ because you want ___, but you get ___ because you ___."

DISCUSSION: The story of Lazarus' resurrection is told once in the Bible but has much to teach. Tell what you took from this story.

My Husband's Thoughts

by Wade Urban

"He who sins is of the devil, for the devil has sinned from the beginning. For this purpose the Son of God was manifested, that He might destroy the works of the devil" (1 John 3:18).

DIVINE HEALING IS A PRIMARY MEANS OF DESTROYING THE WORKS of the devil. As a believer, your mission is the same (see 1 John 4:17). Through Holy Spirit's gifts of faith, gifts of healings, and working of miracles, you're equipped with powerful weapons of warfare to wreak havoc on the enemy's plans to steal, kill, and destroy (see John 10:10). This is an inconvenient truth for many in the body of Christ today. Most, particularly Spirit-filled believers, agree with the concept of healing but rarely experience the reality of God's power. They acknowledge that God *can* heal, but often doubt He'll heal them, let alone use them to heal others.

In this book Connie has described both the legal premise (healing covenant) as well as the vital power (Holy Spirit) to enforce God's will for healing. What remains is experiencing the reality of God's healing power—to heal you and others through you. An experience in Christ's healing power supersedes all doctrines or notes you could ever have about healing. In fact, you're likely educated enough to have your own healing ministry right now! Jesus sent His twelve disciples with power and authority over demons and diseases to preach the gospel of the Kingdom and to heal the sick. Soon afterward, He sent out seventy more with the same mission (see Luke 9:1-2; 10:1-16). They came back with joy and excitement about their experiences, saying even demons were subject to them. Most never realized Jesus sent these eighty-two men out before He ever taught them how to pray (see Luke 11:1-4)! The modern church has become more of a classroom setting of dispensing information than an equipping center training believers through practical experience.

Qualification for ministry certainly includes doctrinal education, but that's never a substitute for God's love and compassion shown through Holy Spirit's gifts in a practical demonstration of destroying the works of disease, sickness, and demonic activity in a person's life. Compassion is the conduit through which Holy Spirit's healing anointing flows. The time has come to return to basics of the gospel of the Kingdom, the power of Holy Spirit in and through believers (see Rom. 14:17). I pray this book will inspire believers to step out in faith and pray for the sick, expecting manifestations of God's covenant promises. I believe the final Great Awakening is on the verge of exploding worldwide; but this won't occur until God's people understand their callings and power of Holy Spirit to save, heal, deliver, and confirm His will with mighty signs and wonders through them (see 2 Cor. 1:20). You've come this far; why not step out in faith right now? If not you, then who? If not now, then when? We live in a target-rich environment with numerous opportunities. You have access to the greatest Power on earth—Holy Spirit. You've been given a destiny and divine purpose greater than just living out your days as merely human (see 1 Cor. 3:3) You're a new creation in Christ Jesus to be a difference-maker.

Afterword

SHORTLY AFTER THE LORD SENT ME ON MY JOURNEY TO WRITE this book, many adversities occurred, most of them related to healing. I became sick, then sicker. Though I prayed and was prayed for, all my faith statements didn't seem to reach the Father's ear. As I said in the prologue, I wondered how He could use me to write a book about healing when healing eluded me. However, after He told me it was a satanic attack because of the book, He urged me onward. Even the following year, as attacks afflicted my husband and me in other ways, I persevered with my assignment. During the ensuing days then weeks then months then years of writing, the Lord revealed and reminded me of many things. As a result I've seen that God allowed those trials to happen for a purpose, and He was doing much in me in the process.

I'd been reared by parents of faith who believed in His healing capabilities despite how everything appeared or the report's severity. Because of their faith walk, I didn't go to a doctor until I was starting kindergarten. He reminded me during the 2016 season of illness that not only were my parents people of faith, but I'm a woman of faith myself. Then, someone lent me a book, *True Stories of the Miracles of Azusa Street and Beyond*, by Tommy Welchel and Michelle P. Griffith. Welchel had interviewed people who witnessed and participated in the Azusa Street revival. Most had been young at the time, but that experience was etched in their minds—cancers falling off, limbs and teeth growing back, deformities being corrected. As a child myself, I'd witnessed similar wonders during the decade of the faith healers of the fifties and sixties. The Azusa Street descriptions made something in me come alive as I recalled also seeing powerful miracles. Like Welchel, those childhood memories had burned into my heart, but I'd let that ember grow cold. Faith for the mega-impossible needed to be rekindled in me.

I also realized that over the years I'd neglected tools I used often for myself and others. I'd gradually overlooked my intense fasting, prayer, and worship time, so I was going unarmed into battle. I needed to prioritize and come to Him first thing each morning. Instead of sitting in my comfy, wing-back chair, feet propped up on my ottoman while sipping my morning's Keurig proceeds, I needed my prayer stance to be continual and sacrificial. I couldn't return to my strong, healthy warrior stance unless I consistently approached Him because intimacy changes things. I also kept mine and others' needs in my prayer partners' hearts and got in multiple prayer lines. I researched scriptures with promises for healing certain ailments, compiled a list, and shared those frequently with others.

God reminded me of my healing heritage and of this scripture: "*Now* faith is..." (Heb. 11:1). Faith brings what's rightfully ours today. Miracles didn't just occur in our distant memory. It's not just for generations past and for us to say wistfully, "I remember when...!" It's faith for *now*. Today! Though God never changes, His way of doing things often does. I needed to build on those old ruins of past movements but make healing a daily reality for me now. I knew I had to finish this book to help myself and others find the faith they've forgotten or maybe never knew. By studying Jesus, I was reminded of my authority against the enemy's curses to derail God's plan for me, and I needed a healthy body for that.

During this book project, I've grown more in love with the Healer and know Him better than ever. I hope you, too, found personal relationship with our Healer as you read His examples and the principles they teach. Sending me on this book journey was not only His healing gift to share with you but also His gift of deeper relationship for me with Him. Today, I'm still awaiting my new spleen from God; in the meantime, I feel stronger than I have in many years. What an amazing Lord, who speaks in ways we can understand and from which we can grow.

Answers to "Questions to Ponder"

Chapter One: Healings and Miracles

1   a.   The man wasn't healed immediately.

     b.   Miracles occur immediately while healings take a while.

     c.   The man first saw men as trees.

     d.   You can't see it at first, but growth has already begun and eventually will come forth. The illness is dying, but symptoms may take a while to leave.

2   a.   Illness is what's wrong in your body. Symptoms are what you feel as a result of the illness.

     b.   When you feel symptoms and say you're not healed, it allows sickness to return.

     c.   Resist, ploys, symptoms, derail, purpose

3   a.   They bring others to the Lord.

b. EXAMPLES: The blind men, lady in the temple who was bent over, deaf man, children, Jairus

c. Kicks power into gear by putting anointing from you as a transfer agent into others

d. Through human hands

4 a. EXAMPLES: Exercise, eat right, use common sense, go to the doctor when necessary

b. EXAMPLES: David and the showbread, Jonathan and honey, Jesus healing on the Sabbath, Jesus and Jairus' daughter's food

c. Doctors and medicines have their place. Often they help with the healing process or make the sufferer more comfortable while healing. You should look to Jesus first and be led by Him about doctors and medicines.

d. The man was looking down (at the dust), and Jesus said to look up.

e. Ahaziah inquired of Baal about his healing before he inquired of God.

5 a. Actions God gives which bring healing

b. EXAMPLES: Slamming a door, washing feet, breaking chains, bursting balloons

c. EXAMPLES: Naaman dipping in the Jordan; Moses stretching his rod over the Red Sea; Joshua marching around Jericho; Jesus spitting on the blind man's eyes, having a man stretch out his hand, spitting on a man's tongue

6 a. Answers will vary.

b.   Originally it was having domestic duties but came to include healing when servants had responsibility for caring for the sick.

c.   He served others, even when He was tired, didn't have healing as a focus that day, or was being arrested.

d.   Peter rashly cut off Malchius' ear. Jesus touched it and healed it.

e.   EXAMPLES: He led them away or healed them before others came around.

f.   Humility

Discussion—answers will vary.

Chapter Two: The Finished Work

1   a.   His death brought both salvation and healing.

b.   *Sozo* means to save, deliver, heal, make whole. When Jesus said the woman was *sozoed,* He did it all.

c.   EXAMPLES: Obedience brings healing, give God the glory, salvation is for all, healing plus salvation came because the leper thanked Jesus.

d.   EXAMPLES: The word *sozo,* the lepers, David says "forgives iniquities, heals diseases," Paul says "prosper, health like the soul."

2   a.   Jesus did the necessary work to assure healing and salvation by His scourging, death, burial, and resurrection.

b.   He changes the verb from "is" to "was," showing it's already done.

c.   His death executed once and for all the payment for your debt of sin.

d. We don't have to ask continually for forgiveness. It's finished.

3 a. Taking one's place as a substitute.

b. Aaron ran through the congregation with a censor to substitute for their sins and judgment. Abraham needed to sacrifice his son for his sin, but God provided a ram in the bush.

c. EXAMPLES: Same—Both F(f)athers offered their sons. God provided His Son as a Ram in the bush. Both were the F(f)athers' *yachids*. Different—God's Son's sacrifice didn't expire. Isaac wasn't sacrificed.

d. Priceless, Son, ultimate, sacrifice, purpose, salvation, healing

e. The first Adam brought death through actions in the Garden. The last Adam brought life through actions on the cross.

f. Grace

4 a. God's presence, the anointing

b. Changes people and brings miracles and salvations

c. Amazed and frightened

d. He and his entire family were saved.

5 a. Pressing in until you have your healing

b. Even though the house was too crowded for the man to go inside, they didn't give up. They took off the roof and let him down.

c. EXAMPLES: The woman with the issue of blood, the Gentile woman with the possessed daughter

6 a. Jesus left so Holy Spirit could arrive and give power to accomplish *greater works* than He did.

    b.   Profitable, helpful, expedient

    c.   Reveals secrets, teaches how to pray when you don't know how, leads in prayer

    d.   When you're saved, you receive Father, Son, and Holy Spirit. After you become *filled* with the Spirit with evidence of speaking in tongues, He becomes activated so you can use His nine gifts.

7   a.   Through angels

    b.   EXAMPLES: An angel told Joseph the Baby was conceived by Holy Spirit. Gabriel told Mary and Zachariah of God's plan. Angels appeared to shepherds and proclaimed the birth. Angels ministered to Jesus in the wilderness and Gethsemane. An angel troubled the waters at Bethesda. He said during His arrest he could call many angels to save Him. An angel rolled away the stone at the tomb.

    c.   38 years

    d.   He didn't recognize Jesus as the Healer and answered Jesus' question about his healing with why He couldn't be healed.

    e.   When Holy Spirit gives a word of knowledge, an angel brings the anointing right then for that particular healing.

    f.   EXAMPLES: Healing, crucial news, help, protection, preparation, revelation of God's will, direction, worship, heavenly homecomings

8   a.   Holy Spirit

    b.   EXAMPLES: Witnessed about Him and did miraculous works, healed at the Gate Beautiful, healed the bedridden man, had great miracles and conversions, healed by Peter's shadow, raised Tabitha and Eutychus

c. Through Holy Spirit

d. He said the healing at the Gate Beautiful wasn't by his power but by God's and told Cornelius not to bow to him because he was just a man.

e. EXAMPLES: To help others without excuses. Religious people aren't always the most compassionate.

9 a. That God's works be revealed

b. No

c. God can't look upon sin. Disobedience opens the door for satan's attacks.

d. EXAMPLES: OT—Psalms, God recompenses by the cleanness of your hands; Proverbs, departing from evil is health to your flesh and if you cover sin, you won't prosper; Isaiah, if you return to the Lord, He'll heal. NT—After He healed him, Jesus told the man at Bethesda to stop sinning or something worse would come on him. Paul says you can't take communion unworthily, and you're promised long life by obeying the commandment to honor parents. James says to confess sins and pray about your health. *More examples will be listed in the chapter "Blocks to Healing."*

e. From the heart

Discussion—answers will vary.

Chapter Three: Faith

1 a. Those who encourage or discourage others from going to Jesus to seek new vision

b. Physical, spiritual

    c.   EXAMPLES: Upsets how they've always done things, may exceed someone else's walk, envy

    d.   Encouragers said to "be of good cheer," brought Jesus' message to him, led him to Jesus, rejoiced for his healing.

    e.   Answers vary.

2   a.   Discouraging words, blindness, beggarly elements, rude crowds, bleeding, over-crowded houses, criticism

    b.   Desperation, afflicted, Jesus', attention, pressing in, results

    c.   EXAMPLES: Wait on God, fall on your face in the secret place, worship, sit in His presence, travail, use Holy Spirits' gifts, pray, fast, call intercessors, don't stop before it's done

    d.   Ask, seek, knock

3   a.   Substance means "setting under, support, essence, assurance, confidence." Faith is your essence and assurance which you should believe and visualize before you see results.

    b.   They waited 25 years; he was 100; Sarah was 90.

    c.   Righteousness

    d.   We have faith that the Bible is God's living Word, that Jesus is God's Son who can take away sins, that God wants to heal us, that healing will be ours.

4   a.   Whatever you speak, they must obey.

    b.   You should believe and to speak the need.

    c.   Solomon says life and death are in the tongue's power. If you speak faith or fear, your healing responds to those words.

    d.   Healing happens more easily when you refuse the illness satan is attempting to give rather than get rid of it after it takes hold.

5   a.   Entreat or beg

     b.   He now wasn't begging for food but for healing. He'd become a victor instead of a victim.

     c.   Jesus stopped to listen.

     d.   What He needed from the Lord

     e.   We don't get because we don't ask. Words have power. We should speak words of faith, not fear.

6   a.   Rise

     b.   God responds to obedience. It changed his perspective to Jesus' perspective and changed his circumstances. It put legs to his faith as he acted on the word of the Lord.

     c.   EXAMPLES: She changed her expression, got up, ate, worshiped, went home.

     d.   EXAMPLES: The ten lepers, Abel, Noah, Abraham, the man at Bethesda, people with Peter's shadow and Paul's cloths, the crippled man at Lystra

7   a.   EXAMPLES: It's tiny, grows rapidly, takes a while to mature, bears fruit, spreads branches wide toward heaven, is large enough to support others.

     b.   EXAMPLES: By reading the Word, praying, experiencing Him, love, trials and testing

     c.   Hearing about God causes a level of faith to arise. When you experience His ability, you know His abilities for certain.

8   a.   EXAMPLES: Shunammite woman, children in the wilderness, Joshua at Jericho, Naaman

     b.   When they came into the Promised Land, each tribe set large rocks up.

c.   Reminders for future generations of where God had brought them from and what He'd done on their behalf.

Discussion—answers will vary.

Chapter Four: Authority

1   a.   He thought he was unworthy for Jesus to come to his house.

    b.   He also operated in love and humility. It was his character, like the centurion.

    c.   He said he was unworthy, but others said he was worthy because he loved Israel and built a synagogue.

    d.   He loved God, prayed regularly, and gave alms to the poor.

    e.   His character is love. He has given much, including His only Son.

2   a.   As a centurion, he had men beneath him. When he told servants or soldiers to do things, they were obligated to do so.

    b.   Since God gave man dominion on earth, Jesus had to come as a man to have legal authority.

    c.   Jesus', authority, everything, nature, sickness, demons, death

    d.   It means "to hear as a subordinate." The centurion's subordinates were obliged to obey.

3   a.   It means force, delegated influence, authority, jurisdiction. It's your power and authority through Jesus.

    b.   Jesus' authority is because the Father is in Him.

    c.   *Exousia* is your authority through Jesus' name. *Dunamis* is the enemy's power.

    d.   Even though the enemy has this strong power, your authority is stronger.

4   a.   His word, His name, His blood

        b.   Both are His word, but the *logos* is His written Word while His *rhema* comes from many sources and gives promises about current situations.

        c.   EXAMPLES: Bible, prophetic word, dream or vision, knowing in your spirit, something you heard or read

        d.   Fire and hammer

        e.   Types of ground

- Nothing can grow or take root. People who don't believe, so satan comes in and steals that seed.

- Stony ground with little dirt, so seed can't withstand the sun. People with weak faith, who become discouraged and lose their healing.

- Among thorns which choked seed out. People who allow others or circumstances to halt their healing.

- Good soil which produces a crop. People with fertile hearts where God can do His healing work.

        f.   Many people read the Word but don't apply those powerful promises to their situations because they've never personally experienced that power.

        g.   *Rhema.* It will cut through situations because it's His *now* word for victory.

5   a.   In Jesus' name

        b.   After healing the lame man, they were arrested and asked what name they came in. Peter told them it was Jesus' name. When they were released, they were told not to speak or teach in His name.

c. No. Later, they prayed for more boldness to speak and perform signs and wonders in His name.

d. They had the opposite of authority. They were trying to exorcise demons in Jesus' name. However, since they weren't Christians, demons refused to recognize their authority and attacked Sceva's sons.

6 a. It's extremely valuable because it's considered that creation's life. Therefore, God required that life to pay for your life.

b. You don't need a high priest because Jesus became your high priest. He was sacrificed once, instead of regularly.

c. From the death angel who brought death to the firstborn

d. Anoint doors and windows to protect homes and families

e. Blood *is haima*, meaning "the atoning blood of Christ." Testimony is *marturia* and means "evidence, record, report." This has a legal connotation. Healing is legally yours.

f. Place of power, authority, protection. Jesus sits there to make intercession so you have authority in His name.

7 a. It's how God deals with man. A sacred, unbreakable promise. God gives you His promise of what He'll do, but it comes with responsibility. It's relationship with Him.

b. EXAMPLES: He covenanted with Abraham, Moses, David, and others.

c. God had made the old covenant with man and required blood. However, it became ineffective. He planned a new, better covenant which also required blood. Jesus' blood fulfilled that requirement.

d. Communion

e.   When Bartimaeus called the second time, Jesus "stood still." The Greek words for both *stood* and *still* mean "covenant, establish." When He stood still to hear Bartimaeus' needs, He made a healing covenant with him.

f.   Since water generally represents Holy Spirit, it was His divinity and humanity mixed together being spilled for you.

g.   God gave a healing covenant at Marah. Jesus' spilled blood and stripes ushered in a new healing covenant. Holy Spirit enforces that covenant through His gifts of healings and miracles.

8   a.   Blood shed unjustly by another

b.   Blood matters to God. The offender's blood must be spilled to repay. Innocent shedding of blood cries out to God, so He exacts vengeance.

c.   EXAMPLES: Cain/Abel, because of sacrifices; David/Uriah, because David impregnated his wife; Joab/Abner and Amasa, because he killed them unjustly; Joash/Zachariah, because he spoke against his idolatry

d.   Jesus' innocent blood

e.   If others' spilled blood moves God to action, what about the innocent blood shed by His only Son?

9   a.   Buying and selling sacrifices for a profit

b.   He grew angry, drove them from the temple, overturned the tables, and didn't allow anyone else to bring goods into the temple.

c.   Like those money-changers, sickness has illegally invaded your temple. You should get angry and drive it out.

d. In love, you should get angry when you see what satan's doing to others and take authority.

Discussion—answers will vary.

Chapter Five: Holy Spirit

1 a. EXAMPLES: Peter's shadow, Paul's garment, Peter's mother-in-law's fever, eyes, ears, tongue, demonic possession

    b. The woman touched Him instead of His touching her.

    c. It's the Greek word for *touch* and means "to attach oneself to." His power attaches itself to you, and healing flows into you.

    d. Through your hands

2 a. Despite her illness which made her unclean, she still approached Jesus and touched His garment.

    b. EXAMPLES: The stigma of uncleanness, shame, past practices, desire to stay in comfort zone, big crowd, public opinion

    c. She said if she could only touch His clothes, she'd become well.

    d. True, wisdom, answer, understanding, heal, unashamedly, worshiping

3 a. EXAMPLES: Helper, Teacher, Prophet, Revealer, Creator of Signs and Wonders, Consuming Fire, Comforter, Counsellor

    b. In that time, He dwelt with them. Now, He dwells in them.

    c. They operate in conjunction with each other. For example, healings (power gift) often occur as a result of a revelation or speaking gift.

4   a.   Words of wisdom, words of knowledge, and discernment of spirits

       b.   EXAMPLES: Unctions, dreams, visions, circumstances

       c.   They give supernatural wisdom and understanding and show how to apply revelations. They reveal future situations.

       d.   When the bird sees the net the enemy spread to snare him, he can avoid that trap. The net is set in vain.

       e.   It allows you to perceive whether a person operates in Holy Spirit, an evil spirit, or flesh.

5   a.   Revelations about past or present events or situations

       b.   When they're revealed, an anointing is present to heal a particular ailment.

       c.   He reveals, heals

6   a.   Prophecy, tongues, interpretation of tongues

       b.   He prophesied under the influence of an evil spirit. He also had in his heart envy, anger, suspicion, displeasure, unforgiveness, and murder. He held a spear in his hand and tried twice to kill David.

       c.   Prophecy

       d.   To avoid confusion and misunderstanding

7   a.   Prayer language doesn't usually lead to prophecy. It typically doesn't occur in a group. It's actually praying instead of giving prophecy. It helps with prayers because Holy Spirit prays when you don't know how to pray.

       b.   When you pray or sing in Holy Spirit's language, He directs you about praying. It brings power and authority.

       c.   Holy Spirit's language

8   a.   Gift of faith, gifts of healings, working of miracles

     b.   More than one way exists to receive them.

     c.   The gift of faith rises up in you along with a surety that it will be done.

9   a.   *Dunamis*

     b.   It comes from Holy Spirit and is unlimited power, force, and ability.

     c.   *Exousia* is the authority of the sheriff's badge. *Dunamis* is the power from his gun.

     d.   A transformer

     e.   It flows from Holy Spirit into the person operating in the gift. As he/she touches another, it leaves him/her and goes into the person who needs healed.

10   a.   It enables you to do signs and wonders through Holy Spirit's ability planted into you to accomplish His purpose.

     b.   Heal emotionally and physically, bring freedom from sin, deliver, preach the gospel

     c.   All things

11   a.   Acting on it

     b.   EXAMPLES: It may seem foolish or not be understood, it has incorrect elements, the receiver may wrongly judge the giver.

     c.   Discouragement or other adverse reactions

     d.   They received gladly then searched Scripture for themselves.

     e.   Saul hated and persecuted Christians. Ananias could be killed by him.

Discussion—answers will vary.

Chapter Six: Healing Tools

1   a.   Jairus was a synagogue ruler. Generally, they hated Jesus.

      b.   He spoke against their religious practices. They were envious of His gifts and popularity.

      c.   His young daughter became ill.

      d.   When his daughter was near death, he knew Jesus had relationship with God, not just religion like his colleagues.

      e.   Bank tellers spot fakes by studying the real thing.

2   a.   Fervent prayers are continually bringing petitions to God and spending time with Him until you receive the answer.

      b.   God honors persistence and answers prayers when you come to Him often.

      c.   EXAMPLES: Fewer distractions, He was replenished, it prepared Him for ministry demands.

      d.   EXAMPLES: He prayed all night before choosing disciples. After intense ministry, He rose early and went to a solitary place. At the Transfiguration, he prayed hard for that event and the intense deliverance that awaited Him the next day.

      e.   It began and ended the drought, made the sacrifice be consumed, allowed him to beat chariots, overcame depression, and made a forty-day journey.

3   a.   Fear

      b.   Believe

      c.   Before, healing, need, deal, fear

      d.   Jesus brought more than sympathy. He brought healing.

4   a.   Those given for impossible needs.

b. Jesus didn't begin the resurrection until those who may have impeded it had left.

c. EXAMPLES: Fear, emotional outbursts, lack of faith, ridicule, unbelief, no focus, negativity, curiosity, distractions

d. He cleared the house.

e. Not being self-centered and staying in a sober mindset

f. Paul was stoned and left for dead. Disciples gathered in one accord and raised him from the dead or nearly dead state.

g. EXAMPLES: Building the church, tongues in the Upper Room, the prison shaking

5 a. Childbirth

b. It's loud, boisterous sobs from deep inside and breaks through the obstacle.

c. He bowed on the ground in prayer then assumed a childbirth position.

d. He wept, groaned in the spirit, and was troubled. The word *pneuma* generally means Holy Spirit. Groans in Romans 8:26 denote grief.

6 a. Travail is often public while fasting is done privately and in humility. Travail is generally for a short period while fasting usually involves a length of time. Travail sweeps over you suddenly while fasting comes through Holy Spirit's leading. Travail generally breaks through sooner than fasting.

b. Esther called the nation to fast before she went before the king. Jehoshaphat called a fast before they faced three huge nations in battle. The king of Ninevah called a fast after Jonah's prophecy.

c. We should fast at His leading because it's individual for each person and each fast. It brings increased Holy Spirit power.

d. When they were unable to cast demons from the son

Discussion—answers will vary.

Chapter Seven: Blocks to Healing

1 a. He ignored her, wouldn't heal her daughter, and called her a dog. She was a Greek, not a Jew, and said healing didn't belong to her.

b. God doesn't hear you if sin is blocking you.

c. EXAMPLES: Naaman, the centurion, this Greek woman's daughter

d. EXAMPLES: Believe, keep asking, be humble, don't react in emotions

2 a. EXAMPLES: The Lord's prayer, Jesus' wilderness temptation, Elijah being fed by ravens and widow, Obadiah feeding prophets.

b. He said it's not good to take the children's bread and give it to dogs. She responded that even dogs could eat crumbs.

c. If a child asks his/her earthly father for bread, he doesn't give him/her a stone. If you ask your heavenly Father for bread (healing), He'll give you what you ask, even more than earthly fathers.

3 a. Faith, fear, Jesus

b. It was a strong demon that caused intense manifestations, including bruising and trying to kill the boy.

c. Jesus didn't scold them for coming to Him but for coming in fear.

4 a. He asked Jesus to help his unbelief.

   b. Jesus heals you and lays you in your Father's arms of love and protection.

   c. In your heart

5 a. All things

   b. Believe

6 a. Prayer and fasting

   b. They slept instead of praying, so they weren't ready for the next day's horrendous events. They all fled, and Peter denied Him.

   c. Sometimes you're unexpectedly called to minister.

   d. EXAMPLES: Shunammite woman with the king; Peter raising Tabitha

   e. Ready in all seasons

7 a. They were suspicious and leery about His miracles and teachings because they knew Him as a child and knew His family.

   b. He could do no mighty works.

   c. A prophet is honored wherever he goes except in his home-town or with his family.

   d. EXAMPLES: You think you're not worthy and are afraid of what others think.

8 a. Fulfill or negate God's promise

   b. A fool's mouth can snare and destroy him, but a wise man's words are like well-driven nails.

   c. She agreed with Jesus, humbled herself by worshiping, then asked Him to help her.

9   a.   EXAMPLES: Pride, lying, murder, devising wickedness, doing evil, sowing discord

      b.   EXAMPLES: Malice, deceit, hypocrisy, envy, lack of submission, disobedience, rebellion, stubbornness, strife, evil

      c.   Rebellion

Discussion—answers will vary.

Chapter Eight: Compassion

1   a.   When the leper said he could be healed if Jesus were willing, Jesus said He was willing.

      b.   He desires, wills, delights in it, and has you on His mind.

      c.   It tells you to present your body as a sacrifice to the Lord. That word means "as a sound whole." God didn't accept sacrifices with flaws.

      d.   He loves you so much He hurts for you even when your misery is your own fault and punishment He's allowed.

2   a.   EXAMPLES: Unclean leper, high priest's servant's ear, feeding multitudes

      b.   Passionate, strong emotions were housed there.

      c.   Compassion, self-centered, focused

3   a.   EXAMPLES: He got sunburned, hot, hungry, weary, thirsty

      b.   He stayed in less-populated areas; got alone and prayed; went to friends' houses for rest, food, and fellowship; kept an escape boat behind him to avoid being crushed by the crowd.

      c.   Intends, balance, wisdom, spiritually, physically

4   a.   Religious leaders

b.   He said if their livestock had fallen into a pit, they'd get it out on the Sabbath. He declared people of more value than animals.

c.   EXAMPLES: Some work against you or rely on you to hear regularly from God for them. That wears you down, impacts confidence, creates distractions, affects sleep, erodes minds and bodies.

5   a.   John the Baptist had died.

b.   EXAMPLE: Hebrews 4:14-15—He sympathizes with your weakness.

6   a.   The mother's son had died, so He raised him.

b.   EXAMPLES: Jairus' daughter, widow of Zarephath (Elijah), and Shunammite woman (Elisha)

c.   Finding a son to care for His mother

Discussion—answers will vary.

Chapter Nine: Deliverance

1   a.   Oppression and possession

b.   EXAMPLES: Supernatural strength, fierceness, foaming at the mouth, wallowing, gnashing teeth, falling to the ground, becoming rigid, falling in fire/water, crying out with a loud voice

c.   No. Jesus asked the name after He told it to come out. He asked to show multiple spirits were present.

d.   Discernment—you should discern in which spirit/Spirit people are operating.

2   a.   EXAMPLES: Viruses, bacteria, weakened immune systems, behavioral problems, etc., can also be a demon at work.

b.   Convulsions, bruising, throwing them down and into fire and water

c.   EXAMPLES: Oppression, violence, crying out constantly and uncontrollably, destructiveness, disturbing stares, saying inappropriate things

d.   The possessed son jumped into fire and water, swine ran over the hill, Judas killed himself.

3   a.   EXAMPLES: Distressing, lying, bondage, etc.

b.   Holiness and wisdom

c.   Fear, trembling, bones shaking, hair on arms standing up

4   a.   Behaviors and practices which allow satanic access

b.   Promises, responsibility

c.   Repentance

d.   You're still tender, weak, and susceptible to the spirit that left. You grow stronger with time.

e.   No. Mary Magdalene had seven and ultimately worked for Him.

5   a.   It makes natural sickness fighters unable to produce, so the body can't go through its natural healing processes. It creates anxiety, which produces substances that change people's actions.

b.   It's like an umbrella that keeps God's blessings from hitting you.

c.   Bitterness

d.   They start easily; grow fast; and are large, numerous, and deep. Though they're difficult to get rid of, they're not impossible.

e.   Difficult, overcome, way, pray, enemies

f.   Sarah conceived.

6   a.   EXAMPLES: Fear, drugs, hypnosis, sexual sin, occult

b.   It's part of satan's territory.

c.   EXAMPLES: Horoscopes, fortune tellers, Ouija boards

d.   Some people still have lifestyles that will attract demons' return. Then it will be seven times worse.

Discussion—answers will vary.

Chapter Ten: Relationship

1   a.   They spent time with Him. He stayed with them, ate, and fellowshipped.

b.   You know each other's characters, habits, personalities, idio-syncrasies, walks with God.

c.   If you take care of the prophets or other men/women of God, you'll be rewarded.

d.   EXAMPLES: Jesus stayed with Peter often, and his mother-in-law was healed; widow of Zarephath gave Elijah food and housing during the drought and got provision and a resurrection; Shunammite woman made a room for Elisha and got a baby and resurrection; Lazarus and his sisters took care of Jesus and got a resurrection.

2   a.   Healing follows Jesus.

b.   Obey, will, glorifies, Himself

c.   He'd been dead four days. People couldn't say it had just worked out.

3   a.   He delayed His trip although his human side probably wanted to rush back to heal His friend.

b.   She didn't go from the house until He called her then rose up quickly and hurried to Him.

c.   Sometimes He asks you to do what seems foolish, but obedience creates great miracles.

4   a.   Mary's friends believed on Jesus and were saved. Others reported it to the Pharisees.

    b.   Lazarus' life testified of Jesus and brought in believers.

5   a.   EXAMPLES: Living right, attending church, helping others, paying tithes, doing devotions, praying

    b.   Martha by waiting on Him; Mary by sitting at His feet

    c.   When Jesus came another time, Martha was still serving, and Mary had grown more in love with Him.

6   a.   Though both know the lord, one seeks deeper intimacy.

    b.   Martha represents religion while Mary represents relationship.

    c.   EXAMPLES: She was stuck in her way of serving the Lord. She criticized Jesus like religion criticizes when others hear from the Lord. Martha didn't really believe Jesus would raise Lazarus. Religion doesn't have experience to know the Lord will perform it. Martha recited doctrine about the resurrection like religion generally understands doctrine. Martha relied on works like many religions think you have to work to get into heaven.

    d.   Thomas doubted unless He saw it instead of having faith. Pharisees were out of touch with God's new season, nor did they recognize His Son and tried to protect their religious empire.

7   a.   EXAMPLES: Be Christ-centered instead of self-centered, spend time with the Lord.

    b.   Relationship, recognize

    c.   John says it was "that Mary." Details are similar elsewhere.

    d.   Resurrection

8   a.   To present yourself as a sacrifice because it's your reasonable service. One definition for the word *service* means "worship."

    b.   She washed His dusty feet.

    c.   She humbly knelt at His feet. She lavished sacrifices on Him. She gave Him what was precious. Worship's scent filled the room.

    d.   Martha's one thing was to serve the Lord by doing. David also wanted one thing—to dwell in God's house. He brought God's presence back to Jerusalem with great celebration and created a tabernacle with continual worship.

    e.   He sent worshippers out front during the battle. He didn't have to fight but just collect the spoils.

    f.   EXAMPLES: Syro-Phoenician woman, leper, Jairus, lady with the issue of blood, ten lepers, Bartimaeus

    g.   Worship, things, things, worship

Discussion – answers will vary.

Notes

Chapter One: Healings and Miracles

1. James Strong, *King James New Strong's Exhaustive Concordance* (Nashville, TN: Thomas Nelson Publishers), G308.

2. Ibid., G2323.

3. Jack W. Hayford, et al., *New Spirit Filled Life Bible*, New King James Version (Nashville, TN: Thomas Nelson, Inc.), "Word Wealth," 1311-1312.

Chapter Two: The Finished Work

1. Strong, G4982.

2. Hayford, "Bottom Note," 1422.

3. Ibid., "Word Wealth," 1416.

4. Strong, G5048.

5. Ibid., G5055.

6. Hayford, "Bottom Note," 1478.

7. Ibid., "Word Wealth," 33.

8. Ibid., "Bottom Note," 936.

9. Strong, G4851.

10. Ibid., G264.

Chapter Three: Faith

1. Strong, G5287.

2. Ibid., G2896.

3. Ibid., G1453.

4. Albert Barnes, "Notes on the New Testament" in *Barnes Notes on the Old & New Testaments* Vol. Matt.-Mark (Grand Rapids, Michigan: Baker Book House, 1981), 145-146.

Chapter Four: Authority

1. Strong, G1654.

2. Hayford, "Word Wealth," 1558.

3. Strong, G1849.

4. Ibid., G3686.

5. Hayford, "Bottom Note," 1495.

6. Ibid., "Word Wealth," 154.

7. Ibid., "Kingdom Dynamics," 154.

8. Strong, G129.

9. Ibid., G3141.

10. Ibid., G3954.

11. *Dictionary of Biblical Imagery,* Leland Ryken, et al., Editors. "Covenant" (Downers Grove, Illinois: InterVarsity Press, 1998), 176.

12. Strong, G2476.

13. Wade and Connie Hunter-Urban, *Your Holy Spirit Arsenal* (Shippensburg, PA: Destiny Image Publishers, Inc., 2018), 140.

Chapter Five: Holy Spirit

1. Strong, G680.

2. Hayford, "Word Wealth," 1498.

3. Strong, G5548.

4. Ibid., G5545.

Chapter Six: Healing Tools

1. Strong, G4151.

2. Ibid., G4726, from G4727.

Chapter Seven: Blocks to Healing

1. F.F. Bosworth, *Christ the Healer* 9th ed. (Grand Rapids, Michigan: Fleming H. Revell), 96.

2. Strong, G5589.

3. Hayford, "Word Wealth," 1512.

4. Bosworth, 20.

5. Hayford, "Word Wealth," 1566.

Chapter Eight: Compassion

1. Hayford, "Word Wealth," 1303.

2. Strong, G4983.

3. Hayford, "Word Wealth," 1317.

4. Strong, G4698.

5. Hayford, "Word Wealth," 1317.

Chapter Nine: Deliverance

1. Strong, G4682.

2. "How Many People with Serious Mental Illness Are Homeless?" Treatment Advocacy Center: Eliminating Barriers to the Treatment of Mental Illness, Arlington, Virginia, 2017, accessed January 5, 2017, http://www.treatmentadvocacycenter.org/evidence-and-research/learn-more-about/3629-serious-mental-illness-and-homelessness.

3. Strong, G169.

4. Lorie Johnson, "The Deadly Consequences of Unforgiveness," CBN News: The Christian Perspective, June 22, 2015, http://www1.cbn.com/cbnnews/healthscience/2015/June/The-Deadly-Consequences-of-Unforgiveness.

5. Barnes, Vol. Luke-John, 120.

Chapter Ten: Relationship

1. Strong, G1392 from G1391.

2. Ibid., G5455.

3. Ibid., G5030.

4. Ibid., G2999.

5. Hayford, "Center Reference," 1370.

About
Connie
Hunter-Urban

CONNIE HUNTER-URBAN GREW UP IN OXFORD, OHIO. HER PARents were Spirit-filled, so she learned early about operating in the gifts of Holy Spirit. She earned a B.S. in English and an M.A. in secondary education from Miami University and taught high school English for 33 years before retiring in 2009. Connie and her husband, Wade, now live in Connersville, Indiana. Having co-founded Restoration Ministries, their goal is to be about the Father's business. During their time in the ministry, Connie and Wade have pastored, evangelized, and taught. Now, she writes and speaks at conferences and churches where she ministers with words of knowledge and prophecy and witnesses many miracles. She and Wade blog online, conduct workshops, host services where others may use their own gifts of Holy Spirit, stream a weekly teaching series, and write and publish a free semi-monthly ministry newsletter. Connie has written several books. Her first published book, *God's Plan for Our Success, Nehemiah's Way,* shows the route of our Christian journey on the way to our God-ordained destiny. Her second book, *The Elijah Anointing,* gleans prophetic principles from Elijah's ministry. Connie's third book, *Your Holy Spirit Arsenal,* which she co-authored with her husband, discusses Holy Spirit's gifts as weapons of warfare. Connie also has a children's book series, *The Josie Adventures.*

CONTACT INFORMATION

Connie Hunter-Urban

P. O. Box 634

Connersville, IN 47331

Phone: 765-825-2030

conniehunterurban@gmail.com

facebook.com/connie.hunterurban

twitter.com/Restor_Ministry